TRI@L,
ERROR,
AND
SUCCESS

ARMINLEAR

TRI@L, ERROR, AND SUCCESS

*10 Insights into Realistic Knowledge,
Thinking,
and Emotional Intelligence*

Sima Dimitrijev, PhD
and
Maryann Karinch

ARMINLEAR

Armin Lear Press
825 Wildlife
Estes Park, CO 80517

Table of Contents

Author's Note *from Sima Dimitrijev* I

Introduction: *Why Switch from Proven Science to Trial and Error?* 5

Part A: The Knowledge Level

1 Laws of Science and Math Are Overgeneralization Traps 25

2 No Process Can Avoid Unpredictable Events 45

3 More of the Same Works in Stable Conditions 65

4 Differences are the Key When the Conditions Change 79

Part B: The Intelligence Level

5 Think by Analyzing Differences before Generalizing Similarities 93

6 Learn from Others but Use the Knowledge Prudently........................... 119

7 Think About Risk and Benefit to Make Free-Will Decisions 141

Part C: The Emotional-Intelligence Level

8 Minimize Risk and Maximize Opportunities by Working in
Holistic Teams.. 165

9 Build Teams on the Platform of Emotions 183

10 Utilize Brain Plasticity to Improve Your Emotional Intelligence 199

Acknowledgements 217

Author Bios.. 219

Endnotes 223

AUTHOR'S NOTE

from Sima Dimitrijev

My physics and math education has been similar to yours in one important aspect: Our teachers have trained us to take for granted the certainty inherent in the laws of physics and math. The elegance of these laws captivated me so much during my secondary education that my heart was telling me to enroll in a physics degree. Instead—motivated to get out of my poor village—I caved in to better employment prospects by enrolling in electronic engineering.

During my five-year degree, I studied high-level science and math along with engineering courses. With time, I began to see the certainty and the absolute precision of the laws of physics as slippery idealizations.

A repulsive example is the conclusion by some scientists that traveling back in time is possible because the fundamental laws of physics are reversible. Based on this conclusion, a time-travelling rocket would be a far more exciting and effective project than Elon Musk's rockets. However, the reversible "laws" of physics are also deterministic, which implies that these timeless laws control us and there is nothing we can do to change the destined travels!

Celebrated minds could not see a problem with the idea of timeless laws, but I am sure you can distinguish the determined past from the uncertain future.

In **Chapters 1 and 2** of this book, we will show you that the experimental "proofs" of eternal laws, including the laws of physics, ignore the uncertainty of random events. A winning lottery ticket does prove that the person who selected the winning numbers was 100 percent correct, but this certainty is about the past and is unrelated to the future. You would not overgeneralize this event as a proof that this person is an expert who can predict the numbers in future draws, but subtle proofs can mislead you. The insights from Chapters 1 and 2 will tune your skepticism, alerting you to disguised overgeneralizations of irrefutable past experience.

I worked in industry after graduation, but I also continued my formal education, earning my Master of Science and PhD degrees. This took me to an academic career, which has involved many research projects, funded by industry, governments, and venture-capital investors. Although this type of research requires expertise, the fundamental research method is trial and error. I am aware of the stigma that people attach to this method, but I can also see how everything in nature evolves by trial and error—from the physical processes that create order out of quantum chaos, through evolution in biology, to how humans learn and think. Trying is the only way to benefit from uncertainty, and I had to do it for a living. With this mindset, I do not hesitate to try new ideas and I do not feel the pressure to persist with plans that are not working. Running research experiments, I do feel good when the expected results confirm my expertise, but I learn the most from experiments with surprising outcomes.

In **Chapters 3 and 4**, we explain the universality of trial-and-error processes to provide you with a good reason to admit your "errors" so that you and others can learn from them.

Chapter 5 describes how this learning happens by using the errors as feedback for improved new trials. Specifically, it shows that reflective thinking is a mental trial-and-error process with two types of feedback loops, different from the straightforward application of knowledge that we discuss in **Chapter 6**.

Turning to the future in **Chapter 7**, we show how thinking and knowledge help us understand the risks in the uncertain future and, consequently, help us make free-will decisions which risks to take.

A risk I do not take is to share my first-draft sentences with others, even though I do think before I write them down. However, having published many research papers with co-authors, I've seen how our writing crystallizes when we share drafts and provide each other with as critical feedback as possible. It's never easy to receive negative feedback, but we know that it's much easier to deal with critical comments by colleagues than to deal with a rejection of a submitted paper because the reviewers didn't understand it. To emphasize the positive aspect of this process, I call it "collective thinking."

When I started working on this book, I wanted to get some no-nonsense feedback from someone who was familiar with writing for the general audience. It seemed the model of publishing trade books through literary agents would provide me with sufficient feedback to shape this book and make it useful to the general reader. The strongest interest I received was from the leading non-fiction agents, but their responses were awakening me to the reality that these agents were too busy for the detailed engagement that this book required. Then I came across Maryann Karinch, the founder of The

Rudy Agency, and her unusual model of co-authoring books for the general readership. Her expertise in interpersonal skills complemented very nicely the insights I was seeking to convey, and her interest in helping people matched my motivation for writing this book. It didn't take us long after my initial contact to decide that we could make a very effective team as co-authors. To ensure this would be so, Maryann wrote the following sentences in one of her early e-mails to me: "We must be straightforward with each other. Clearly, you will need to change things I've done and I will want to change things you've done! We have enough EQ to do this well, I'm sure!"

When generalized to activities beyond writing, this advice summarizes the messages from Chapters 8, 9, and 10, which discuss the emotional intelligence needed to benefit from collective application of the trial-and-error method. As you can infer from Maryann's sentences, the idea of collective work is to share and integrate diverse knowledge so to create more than the sum of individual contributions.

Describing this holistic effect, **Chapter 8** shows the difference between the organization of holistic groups and the hierarchical organization where you have to do things exactly as the boss tells you. In **Chapter 9**, we discuss the emotions that can either pull people apart or bring them together into holistic groups. Finally, **Chapter 10** shows how holistic moral values improve the emotional intelligence and, consequently, strengthen collective trials.

I hope that this brief chapter overview, in the context of my personal story, illustrates the underlying narrative that it takes (a) *realistic* knowledge, (b) thinking intelligence, and (c) emotional intelligence to deal with and benefit from uncertainty.

INTRODUCTION

Why Switch from Proven Science to Trial and Error?

We know that the future will be different from the past. To deal with this uncertainty, we turn to experts whose knowledge can help us make the best decisions. As statistician and risk analyst Nassim Nicholas Taleb described in *Fooled by Randomness,*[1] even venture-capital investors like to follow proven formulas to manage their investment risks. Sometimes we are worried about specific bits of advice and seek a second opinion. We can get away with that as customers but, as employees, we can rarely seek a second opinion from another supervisor. Moreover, we may feel impotent when doubting ideas that reputable experts support by mathematical modeling. People trust the math apparatus, especially when the experts use it with links to the exact sciences.

A striking example of people's trust in math models is how the world reacted to the unknown coronavirus that was spreading from the Chinese city of Wuhan at the beginning of 2020. The new virus created a fear of uncertainty. To deal with this fear, people turned to scientists who offered advice and predictions. An epidemiological model from the Imperial College London, a respected public research university, played into peoples' desire for certainty. As one of the most influential models, it had a decisive impact on the world's response to the coronavirus. This model projected that—under the unmitigated scenario—more than two million people would die in the United States and more than half a million would die in the United Kingdom within two to three months. In the summary of the paper, the authors stated that "optimal mitigation policies" might reduce deaths by half.[2] As shocking as these projections were, they implied an unusual behavior of the unknown virus. It should be common sense that modeling of unknown behavior cannot be "certain science," but that didn't alleviate people's fear caused by the projected deaths.

On the other hand, it was quite certain that prolonged lockdowns would lead to severe economic damage. However, we didn't have models predicting the number of deaths due to this devastation of businesses around the world. Also, these deaths would happen in a distant future and most people didn't fear them—they feared the near-term threat.

The epidemiological models provided the only "certainty" about the imminent future. So it seemed the only reasonable option was to accept and implement an unprecedented lockdown of people that was certain to wipe out tens of millions of jobs.

In addition to all of that, mathematical models in economics are not as trusted as epidemiological models. Thinking that way, let's take another step to have a look at the most trusted math, which formulates the laws in physics. In this context, Newton's second law of motion is a classic example to illustrate a problem with this trust. Newton's first law addresses forces in balance; the second law describes how objects behave when all forces are not balanced. A general and a logical prediction based on this second law, the law of acceleration, is that a relatively small force is needed to accelerate *any* light car—regardless of specific differences in color, engine type, body shape, tire pressure, and so on. Surprisingly, this prediction includes a light car with deflated tires! The trick here is that the force in Newton's law is the total force, defined as the difference between the engine force and the opposing friction. This is indeed a trick because the friction force—due to either a tire burst or any other factor—is unpredictable. In practical terms, the generality of Newton's law is limited to ideal frictionless conditions, which ignore the fact that friction is responsible for more than 50 percent of the fuel consumption.

It's unwise to disparage the simplicity of this insight. We want you to see that the inability of such a general law of physics to predict a tire burst is surprisingly similar to the inability of economic models to predict events such as the extent to which businesses collapsed due to a virus. We want you to know that the widespread illusion about the absolute generality of the laws of physics works for two reasons: (1) their mathematical formulation resonates with people's desire for certainty and (2) their inherent idealizations make them elegant.

The elegance of idealized laws captivates science away from reality. This problem is not limited to exact sciences. Riskless business models are just as alluring as the frictionless models in physics. The dream is to kick a business off and to watch it move forward forever, just as a kicked ball should roll smoothly in perpetuity according to Newton's first law (that is, an object in motion stays in motion unless something stops it). The scientist in us likes these idealized models even if they are not useful, which Richard Feynman, a theoretical physicist and Nobel laureate, explained in the following way: "Science is like sex: sometimes something useful comes out, but that is not the reason we are doing it."[3]

Of course, it's good when science creates a useful surprise. However, idealized laws, absolute logic, and perfect symmetries are platonic concepts that are not only different from real sex but also sometimes lead to unhelpful surprises. Although empirical knowledge about specific friction forces is not scientifically elegant, engineers must use it to design reliable cars, because no surprise on the road is elegant.

Agreeing that better *factual* knowledge means fewer surprises, the question now is whether the most knowledgeable expert should be the most trustable. According to the French scholar Pierre-Simon Laplace, there could be no surprises for an intellect able to "comprehend all the forces by which nature is animated and the respective situation of the beings who compose it."[4] For such an intellect, nothing is uncertain; the future is predictable. The absolute lack of surprises for this conceptual intellect—known as Laplace's demon—is an implication of a centuries old principle that everything must have a reason or a cause.

However, the following joke illustrates a blind spot of Laplace's knowledge demon—that is, some things in the future are unknowable:

> An old teacher and a bored computer geek are waiting for their flight that's been delayed. To break the boredom, the geek suggests to the teacher: "Let's play a game. I'll ask you a question and if you don't know the answer, you'll give me five dollars. Then you'll ask me a question and if I don't know the answer, I'll give you five dollars."
>
> The teacher replies, "No way. That's not fair. You can use your computer to access information on the internet."

The geek is not giving up: "Well, we can make it fair. If I don't know an answer, I'll give you a hundred dollars. If you don't know an answer, you'll give me five dollars."

The teacher agrees, and the geek asks the first question: "What is the distance between the Earth and the Moon?"

Without even trying to answer, the teacher gives a five-dollar bill to the geek and asks her question: "What was Einstein's most dangerous idea?"

The geek starts searching for the answer on his computer, but neither Google nor his databases can help. Eventually, and reluctantly, he gives a hundred dollars to the teacher. After some silence, the geek asks: "So, what is the answer?"

Giving another five-dollar note to the geek, the teacher answers: "Don't know."

The teacher stepped beyond knowable facts to play the game: "Don't know" was the teacher's answer that enabled her to win this knowledge game. On the other hand, the geek overvalued his superior access to facts and, crucially, he proposed the model of unequal payments because he didn't see the winning effect of asymmetry from his scientific perspective.

The deep-rooted moral of the joke is this: Better knowledge does mean fewer surprises, but the mindset behind Laplace's demon overgeneralizes "better knowledge" to "perfect knowledge" and "fewer surprises" to "absolutely no surprises." The idea that all future events are predictable because they are perfectly tied to knowable past events is an overgeneralization. *The future is neither perfectly predictable nor perfectly uncertain.*

Here is an example of neither perfectly predictable nor perfectly uncertain outcomes: Random gene mutations have evolved into a large variety of unpredictable organisms, but it is quite certain that only those with wings can fly. Unsurprisingly, both birds and airplanes have wings. Moreover, the purpose-driven method that humans apply to design airplanes is similar to Darwin's natural selection of birds. The biggest difference is the ability of humans to perform air-crash investigations, and to use the results as feedback for improved subsequent trials. This difference is not a replacement for, but a very effective upgrade of the evolutionary method.

Evolutionary biologist Richard Lewontin described Darwin's theory of evolution by the words "trial and error" and stated that this was one of only a few great ideas in the history of human thought.[5] Max Born—another Nobel laureate in physics—explained that scientists also work by trial and error, because there are no roads in science with signposts to the future:

"... we are in a jungle and find our way by trial and error, building our road *behind* us as we proceed. We do not *find* signposts at crossroads, but our own scouts *erect* them, to help the rest."[6]

Although not using the words "trial and error," Feynman describes how the physicists use this method to create the laws of physics:

In general, we look for a new law by the following process. First, we guess it. Then we compute the consequences of the guess to see what would be implied if this law that we guessed is right. Then we compare the result of the computation to nature, with experiment or experience, compare it directly with observation, to see if it works. If it disagrees with experiment, it is wrong. In that simple statement is the key to science. It doesn't make any difference how beautiful your guess is. It doesn't make any difference how smart you are, who made the guess, or what his name is—if it disagrees with experiment, it is wrong. That's all there is to it.[7]

We use a law of chemistry to grow moissanite—a silicon-carbide based jewel, considered a diamond alternative, but with higher indexes for brilliance, "fire," and luster than diamond. To grow this crystal, we supply silicon and carbon atoms by mixing certain gasses at certain pressures in a heated furnace. Setting this growth condition is all we can do. We cannot order the gas molecules to follow Newton's laws of motion and to deliver silicon and carbon atoms directly to their positions in the crystal. The molecules fluctuate randomly and the first structures they make on the surface of the growing crystal are crap. Ernest Hemingway's remark, captured in the memoir published by his deck hand Arnold Samuelson, that "the first draft of anything is shit" is a metaphor for this chemical process. The atomic structures that do not fit in the crystal order are short lived, just as the messy word structures disappear when the sentences are revised. It takes many short-lived attempts before the random shuffling of silicon and carbon atoms locks them into the stable structure of the growing crystal. Therefore, the following conclusion is the same, whether we think of crystals or sentences: *The beauty of gems is not made by elegant processes but by the messy trial-and-error method.*

As a general metaphor, this reflects the main premise of the book: Nature is not *governed* by perfect laws of physics; it *evolves* by trial-and-error processes.

This insight matters because the widespread belief in laws, principles, formulas, and processes that ignore randomness leads to overgeneralizations, wrong expectations, and subsequent surprises. To avoid this trap, we need to understand very clearly that our decisions and actions are trials with varying chances of success and then to learn how to improve the chances. In other words, *we need knowledge for the smartest possible implementations of the trial-and-error method.*

We need much smarter implementations than in the

infinite monkey theorem, which the Wiktionary describes as "the proposition that a monkey hitting typewriter keys at random is bound to produce meaningful text (like a work of Shakespeare), given an infinite amount of time." Of course, the need for infinite time turns this theorem into a joke. Nonetheless, people take seriously its oversimplified view of random trials. An example is Andreas Wagner's analysis in his *Arrival of the Fittest*. Wagner reveals that the finite time since the big bang was not sufficient for the 20 amino-acid "letters" to line up randomly in a specific string of only 100 "letters"—a protein that is analogous to a 100-letter sentence rather than to a complete work by Shakespeare.[8] This is Wagner's numerical proof of Hugo de Vries's opinion that "natural selection may explain the survival of the fittest, but it cannot explain the arrival of the fittest." However, Wagner's proof is limited to the monkey-and-keyboard implementation of the trial-and-error method. Hemingway and Feynman's implementations are different. The atomic trial-and-error process that grows crystals is also different.

This book presents the trial-and-error processes that work at three levels:

Level A—*the knowledge level*—highlights differences between the certainty in exact sciences and the uncertainty in reality, with the aim of demonstrating how everything in nature evolves by trial and error.

Level B—*the IQ level*—shows how you can employ mental trial-and-error processes with feedback as efficient thought experiments (sometimes in a combination with real-life experiments but always in a combination with existing knowledge).

Level C—*the EQ level*—deals with interpersonal trial-and-error behavior in holistic groups that survive and prosper by sharing knowledge and ideas.

The trial-and-error processes, presented at these three levels, do not offer recipes but rather develop ten overarching insights, which correspond to each of the ten chapters in the book. The aim is to help you spot uncertainty in "proven" formulas and advice based on irrefutable past evidence and, subsequently, to show you how to combine efficient thinking and emotional intelligence to deal with and even benefit from the identified uncertainty.

But putting aside pure luck, how is it possible to benefit from uncertainty?

The following simple scenario links the ten overarching insights from each chapter, as it illustrates how they can help you pinpoint the crux of uncertainty and then turn it into a desirable outcome.

Your company is launching a new line of healthy sauces and must reduce production and distribution costs to compensate for the increased cost of organic ingredients (a key feature). Your boss hired a consultant who recommended streamlining the production and distribution process by a complex fabrication-on-demand system. Everything would be automated by full computer control. It involves collecting data about the actual demand in supermarkets and restaurants, and then processing the data as feedback to ensure there is neither shortage nor oversupply of specific sauce varieties. The consultant's advice is to combine past sales data with predictions of future trends based on customer profiling and data obtained from various platforms. The consultant says computers can perform all data processing, meaning no expense for additional employees.

Your job is to lead the development of computer software to implement the recommended automation. But your nonsense antenna is alerting you to problems in the consultant's advice. There are two options in this conflict situation:

1. Ignore your doubt and do your best to implement the recommendation. You need a compliant mindset for this do-as-you-are-told option, so you could focus on relevant knowledge that others applied to similar tasks. This option is strictly according to the management system of top–down requests and bottom–up responses.

2. Focus on the differences between reality and the consultant's ideas. Reality is that the future is not perfectly predictable, which is different from the belief that adequate information can eliminate disruptive and costly shortage of materials, production jams, oversupply of products, and so on. With a focus on this difference between reality and the consultant's ideas, you can crystallize your doubt. You can get clarity needed to honor your gut reaction that says, "Don't do it that way!" Then, you'll be able to ask specific questions and to discuss task modifications in a professional way—using knowledge-based arguments and emotional intelligence so that the boss and the consultant will not see your suggested changes as a disruptive negative feedback.

The second option, which involves a kind of "manage-up" element, is your chance for a big win. However, it requires your engagement with the perceived uncertainty. The following ten insights will guide you through this engagement.

A. THE KNOWLEDGE LEVEL

Insight 1: Laws of Science and Math Are Overgeneralization Traps.

The do-as-you-are-told option

A streamlined flow of data for a seamless control of the production and distribution process is the best-case scenario for the proposed fabrication-on-demand system. Computers can process data, but you need adequate equations, which programmers can turn into the requested software. You contract science and math experts to help your group develop the mathematical model. The experts derive the needed equations using proven calculus theorems, which have been used to develop all other process models, ranging from economics to fundamental physics. The equations correspond to the best-case scenario of a perfectly streamlined process, so there is nothing to worry about if you are taking the do-as-you-are-told option.

The alternative

In contrast, you learn in Chapter 1 that *the idea of a perfectly streamlined process is a dangerous overgeneralization.* The reason is random fluctuations, which the "law of large numbers" does not always remove (contrary to the widespread belief that the behavior of a large number of people is predictable even if the behavior of a specific person is unpredictable).

With this knowledge, you can see that random fluctuations will lead to both unpredictable expenses due to oversupply and, even worse, loss of valuable customers due to undersupply. In general, this knowledge will fine-tune your skepticism about the how-to advice you're hearing from colleagues, consultants, or the boss.

Insight 2: No Process Can Avoid Unpredictable Events.

The underlying problem is not limited to the psychology and unpredictability of people. Chapter 2 shows that the problem is fundamental because *eventless processes* do not exist. An eventless process is a perfectly smooth or continuous process, devoid of any disruption by unexpected events. Ignoring the likelihood of unexpected events seems crazy, but people do it all the time in both business and science.

Because you contracted science and math experts to develop the process model you need, it's good to know that their equations will be "blind" for any disruption by unexpected events. The fundamental reason for that is their use of calculus—the mathematics of *continuous change* invented by Gottfried Leibniz and Isaac Newton—which is inconsistent with the concept of random events.

Insight 3: More of the Same Works in Stable Conditions.

Highlighting that only *rare* random events can be disruptive, Chapter 3 shows how replications of random events create the predictability and the order that scientists describe as laws. Your take-away from this is "don't overgeneralize the concept of random events." In other words, don't assume that unpredictable and disruptive events will happen frequently. The useful approach is to keep doing what has worked in the past, *but only as long as the relevant conditions remain stable.*

Insight 4: Differences Are the Key When the Conditions Change.

The only certainty about the future is that the current conditions will change. Chapter 4 describes why this is so and why *trial and error is the only method that is adaptable to unpredictable changes.* So even the most sophisticated rigid methods will fail. This is in line with the overarching principle of evolution—it is not the strongest or the most intelligent who will survive, but rather those who can best manage change.

This insight takes you to an ah-ha moment: Any fixed process model, no matter how complex and detailed, will fail in the future even if it worked well in the past. You realize that you have to think carefully how to modify the request for an automatic control of the production and distribution process.

The insights at the intelligence level in the following chapters will improve the efficiency of your thinking.

B. THE INTELLIGENCE LEVEL

Insight 5: Think by Analyzing Differences before Generalizing Similarities.

Science experts validate their mathematical models by demonstrating an acceptable fit to available data. (My sort-of square peg will fit into your sort-of round hole...) Believing in conceptual perfection of a developed model, they ignore the differences from what they consider noisy data. The term we use to describe the effect of ignored differences is "generalization of similarities." The key insight in Chapter 5 is that you should spot and analyze suspicious differences before you dismiss them as irrelevant. Some differences will turn out to be relevant and they will guide you to make changes in your conceptual model and to try again.

Your thinking is a trial-and-error process with feedback loops that guide you to create a new model (new knowledge) as you try to find a match to the changing reality.

Rigid algorithms cannot perform the key thinking element—the analysis of differences—because some differences are irrelevant in some conditions but become relevant when the conditions change (and some future changes are unpredictable). You could implement self-learning algorithms, but machine learning is different from human learning. In terms of the need to analyze unknown circumstances, the most important difference is that humans learn by communicating and sharing knowledge. This thinking turns into a light-bulb moment. It sparks the idea for a hybrid human–computer model. Humans will have to analyze any unusual changes in the data. Instead of processing these changes, without the ability to adapt, the software can simply tag them as new events for human consideration. The implication is that humans will have to be involved in any workable implementation of the request to minimize cost by a streamlined production and distribution process.

Insight 6: Learn from Others but Use the Knowledge Prudently.

Chapter 6 shows how to use similarities with existing knowledge to support your thinking and decision making, while avoiding the trap of overgeneralizing these similarities. For example, your idea to combine human analysis with computer processing is similar to past implementations of the hybrid man-and-machine model. You recognize similarities with PayPal's use of a hybrid model to prevent credit-card fraud in their transactions—a model that saved the PayPal project. It helps to know that Peter Thiel, a co-founder of PayPal and Palantir, considers the human–computer hybrid approach as a core principle. He describes in his book *Zero to One* that this principle guided him to cofound Palantir on the following idea: "use the human–computer hybrid approach from PayPal's security system to identify terrorist networks and financial fraud."[9] You could also find similarities with Elon Musk's failure to utilize fully automated assembly line for the promised cost reduction and increase in production capacity of his Tesla Model 3 electric car. Admitting that "excessive automation at Tesla was a mistake," he tweeted his realization that "Humans are underrated."[10] You would have missed what Thiel and Musk learned and found valuable if you had adopted, ignoring your doubts, the do-as-you-are-told option of implementing the recommended full automation.

Insight 7: Think about Risk and Benefit to Make Free-Will Decisions.

Popularity of Sam Harris's book *Free Will* shows people's engagement with the silly idea that their free will is just a convincing illusion. This engagement makes it easier for these people to abandon their free will by selecting the do-as-you-are-told option. By not seeing any risk in this option, people cannot see that a free-will decision for a better alternative is possible.

Chapter 7 explains how understanding the risks of all your options enables you to make a free-will decision of which risk to take.

In our example, you would have to estimate the risk of telling the boss openly that your insights and ideas do not fully agree with the consultant's recommendation and, consequently, the risk of suggesting a departure from the request for a fully automatic control of the streamlined process. Then you can compare the risk of this alternative with the risks of other options, including the option to fully comply with the original request.

You need the insights from the emotional-intelligence level for adequate risk estimates and comparisons of the available options.

C. THE EMOTIONAL-INTELLIGENCE LEVEL

Insight 8: Minimize Risk and Maximize Opportunities by Working in Holistic Teams.

Imagine you ask the boss to modify the initial request and the response is positive, but under the condition that you would be responsible for any problem the hybrid approach may create. Accepting full responsibility for the implementation of your idea, you would be taking unnecessary risk.

The insight in Chapter 8 is about creating and working in holistic groups, so that you can both minimize the risk and take opportunities arising from uncertainty. Specifically, you need to see that knowledge communication in holistic groups is not limited to the simple top–down flow of requests and bottom–up flow of responses. There are elements of "managing up" in holistic teams. This happens when employees deal with doubtful expertise in a way that initially looks disruptive but eventually preempts unresolvable conflicts. However, you should keep in mind that unjustified bottom–up requests do not work.

In our example, you will need to do a lot more than simply ask for a modification of the initial request so that you can try your idea. You have to try your best to explain both the problem with the original request and your new idea, and to do so in a way that will entice the boss to own together with you the new hybrid approach. That way, not only will you share the risk but also the boss's contributions will ensure that you will achieve much better outcome together than what you could achieve on your own.

Insight 9: Build Teams on the Platform of Emotions.

Emotions can either pull people apart or bring them together into holistic groups—and Chapter 9 explores the mechanics of those dynamics. The facial expressions of these emotions have evolved as a communication method that we inherited from our predecessors, so it is almost impossible to hide the facial expressions of certain key emotions.

When you present a new radical idea to your manager or team, it will surprise them, but you may also see signs of fear, anger, or disgust. That will tell you to move quickly to explain your idea. If you notice fear, you should know that people begin to see a danger in your proposal. You need to deal with this sign immediately, explaining why your approach reduces the risk for the whole team. If you notice signs of anger, your manager is preparing for a fight over the idea. You still have a chance to turn the situation around if you could understand the specific exclusive right that he wants to protect. Disgust or contempt indicate a total lack of desire to get involved with your ideas.

Eventually, the new idea may elicit a welcoming and easily recognizable happiness. You may also entice a more positive response than the one you got initially. You have more control than you may have imagined. Any positive response is your signal to take action and move forward.

Insight 10: Utilize Brain Plasticity to Improve Your Emotional Intelligence

Almost instinctively, either from the tone of written sentences or from facial expressions, we begin to form a view whether to trust another person. As a test, we may ask surprising questions or make surprising statements to see another person's reactions.

Chapter 10 shows that your moral values guide your basic emotions, which are extremely difficult to hide for most people. For example, if your moral value is to have the exclusive ownership of your new approach, the boss will see it and you may not be able to get the help you need to execute it. That is why this chapter illuminates how to use the gained holistic insights to develop holistic moral values that will guide your emotional reactions; in other words, how you can improve your emotional intelligence.

With earned trust, you are the big winner: You will implement the hybrid model together with your colleagues and supervisor, save money for the company, and get promoted (or even attract funding for a new company, as Thiel did after the PayPal's success with the hybrid model).

With the do-as-you-are-told approach, you will be blamed when the fully automated system fails. Knowing this, you should start looking for a new job if you fail to convince the boss that the consultant's advice is problematic.

PART A

The Knowledge Level

1

Laws of Science and Math Are Overgeneralization Traps

Benjamin Franklin famously said in a 1789 letter to French physicist Jean-Baptiste Le Roy that "in this world nothing can be said to be certain, except death and taxes." In modern times, we know of some people who've successfully evaded taxes—at least for a while—so we might restrict the only certainty in life to "death," bearing in mind that its timing is not set.

With that in view, we begin a dive into the role of unpredictability in your success. In a world where algorithms dominate certain types of decision making, you might think we're either heretics or idiots. Not so! We are here to help you see that shying away from trial and error—in admiration of untainted logic and adherence to laws of science and math—doesn't yield the best results. And we will explore how that happens. Inherent in our thinking is this view: A professional in any field who rejects skepticism to rely on the certainty of math and laws of science when making decisions is a fool.

An elegant physics once misled a business strategy.

In the days of the first personal computers, the semiconductor industry was using ultra-violet light to "print" millions of tiny features on each microchip. However, functionality of these microchips and computers was primitive in comparison to today's smart phones. Many more and much smaller features were needed to enable more powerful microchips but, according to all experts at the time, the reduction of feature sizes by the use of light was approaching the ultimate physical limit.

The physical limit was the wavelength of light (physics tells us that light is a wave and, just as in the case of water waves, the distance between two adjacent crests or troughs is the wavelength). Believing the wave interpretation and modeling of light behavior, the experts reached the following firm conclusion: Light cannot create a narrower line than its wavelength, period.

To move beyond this physical limit, many companies and governments invested a lot of money into development of microchip "printing" by X-rays. One of these investors was Hoya—a large Japanese company with expertise in advanced optics technologies. Hoya's managers saw an opportunity for almost certain success. With wavelengths at least twenty times shorter than ultra-violet light, X-rays were the next available option in the radiation spectrum. Machines that generate X-rays were available, but commercial masks needed for the "printing" were missing. With adequate investment, Hoya's engineers developed a new material and technology, and the company was ready to offer X-ray masks as their new product.

Surprisingly, the need for this product did not evolve. The semiconductor industry continued to use ultra-violet light. They broke the apparent physical limit by creating much smaller features on microchips than the wavelength of ultra-violet light!

This was not simply bad luck for Hoya's managers. The experts misled them by overgeneralizing the wave model. Their firm conclusion ignored the fact that light consists of photons as individual and randomly jiggling particles. The observed wave patterns of light in various experiments are idealizations analogous to observed purchase patterns after many customers buy a certain product. This idealization ignores the unpredictability of individual purchase events, analogously to the ignored random jiggling of individual photons by the wave model of light.

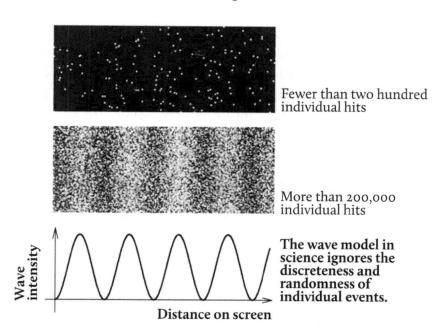

Fewer than two hundred individual hits

More than 200,000 individual hits

The wave model in science ignores the discreteness and randomness of individual events.

Diffraction experiment performed by Akira Tonomura and co-workers at Hitachi in 1989.[11] The photos show where individual particles hit a screen after they pass through two narrow slits.

The analogy with a purchase pattern tells us that, in spite of the existing degree of randomness and unpredictability, individual purchase decisions can be influenced by sales conditions, marketing, and so on. In the example with individual particles of ultra-violet light, engineers changed the conditions by altering the path that each light particle travels through the mask and from the mask to the microchip. This constrained the random paths of individual light particles, shrinking the apparent wavelength of the aggregate wave pattern.

The takeaway here is that the wave equations provide an elegant model for an *averaged behavior* of many particles, but physics overgeneralizes this elegance by ignoring the randomness and the size of individual particles.

The bottom line is that, even if you can stay away from physics and high-tech issues in your everyday life, you need to learn how to distinguish between useful generalizations and harmful overgeneralizations. That's because your knowledge consists of generalizations, but your overgeneralizations turn some of that knowledge into mistaken beliefs. To help you see the roots of these unhelpful beliefs, we will use simple but somewhat shocking examples.

It's all about seeing the limit of generalizations.

We know that generalizations such as "all politicians are hypocrites" and "all investors are greedy" ignore the diversity among politicians and among investors.

When Mark Twain generalized all people into the class of humans in his satirical essay, *The Lowest Animal*, he consciously ignored some differences between people:

> ... the human race is of one distinct species. It exhibits slight variations (in color, stature, mental caliber, and so on) due to climate, environment, and so forth; but it is a species by itself, and not to be confounded with any other.[12]

The differences that matter in Twain's essay are those between humans and all other animals, and he describes religion as one of them:

> Man is the Religious Animal. He is the only Religious Animal. He is the only animal that has the True Religion—several of them. He is the only animal that loves his neighbor as himself, and cuts his throat if his theology isn't straight.[13]

Clearly, the step from religion to *true* religion is a generalization step too far, and yet it resonates with peoples' desire for a perfect clarity and certainty. That's why the idea of true religion has seduced so many smart minds to fight and kill for a futile *overgeneralization* that doesn't recognize religious differences.

Not everyone believes in God, but we all believe in something; and just like the true religion, *true* beliefs are the most common cause of unresolvable disputes. Max Born, the winner of the 1954 Nobel Prize in Physics for his statistical interpretation of the quantum theory of small particles, described this problem in general terms: "The belief that there is only one truth, and that oneself is in possession of it, is the root of all evil in the world."[14]

Yet, you shouldn't rush to brand people with strong opinions as evil. Why would they be evil if they discuss their opinions with open mind, knowing that communication is the key to resolving conflicts and, more generally, the key to success? Quotes about the wisdom of silence seem to be endless, but neither leadership nor education came from the wise people who kept their ideas and opinions for themselves. Moreover, whatever the level of your responsibilities, keep in mind the following quote attributed to Albert Einstein: "If I were to remain silent, I'd be guilty of complicity."[15]

With this mindset, Einstein did not gloss over his

disagreement with Max Born's attack on the idea of unique truths. Born's pioneering work originated the idea that at the elementary level nature and the universe are random, with events happening purely by chance. Einstein chastised him: "God does not play dice," he told Born in a 1926 letter. Where Born's work indicated chaos and randomness as the key factors in creating our world, Einstein saw the order and rationality of nature and the universe.

The implications of Born's work do not contradict the order we observe and the certainty of some predictions. For example, we trust the experts when they predict solar eclipses, and we consider the relevant laws and order as irrefutable scientific truths. However, this specific example shouldn't make you accept that calculations of the Earth's *average* temperature, with the precision of about 0.1 degree Celsius, are irrefutable scientific truths. The Earth's *average* temperature is a climate-defining generalization, which disregards the hundreds of times larger temperature variations—across different regions and over time—as weather fluctuations.

Analogously, the financial managers ignore market fluctuations to present and predict market trends. Do you believe they know which fluctuations to ignore? Whom should we believe if two experts ignore different fluctuations to present different irrefutable truths? As observed by Twain and Born, this is the cause of most serious conflicts.

The philosophy of *complete* law and order is a fertile ground for cultivating conflicting true beliefs; therefore, we should not be silent about the inherent ignorance of this overgeneralization.

Be aware of the ignorance that creates the general laws of science.

It's foolish to rely on the certainty of exact science because this certainty doesn't translate to the flexibility of biological evolution, cognition, and creativity. Of course, we are not saying that the laws of science are useless. We know how professionals use these laws and how educators teach you to use them for specific tasks. Our aim is to help you see the intellectual gap between the exact science and the real world—no matter what you've heard from various experts.

Take the concept of a carbon atom as a fundamental example. The laws of physics and chemistry assume all carbon atoms as identical, but that's not true. Atoms are not static objects with identical shapes, because the electrons, protons, and neutrons of each atom exhibit random jiggling. Scientists ignore this random behavior when they present the theory that all carbon atoms obey the same general laws of physics and chemistry, but you wouldn't know this by reading textbooks.

Trusting the textbooks, you'd be right to expect that the laws of physics should pack carbon atoms into identical diamond crystals. And, as expected, diamonds cut in the same shape and labeled with the same price in a jewelry shop do look identical, but only because we don't see the positions of individual atoms in the crystal grains. In reality, every diamond grain has its own distribution of inevitable defects in the atomic order. These random crystal defects are differences that make every single diamond grain unique, just as the random fluctuations are differences that make every carbon atom unique.

Science has to ignore irrelevant differences to create general concepts, and we are not going to say that these generalizations are not useful. Of course they are. It's helpful to classify many diamond jewels as an identical product. That way, we can distinguish diamond from the cheaper moissanite—a crystalline mixture of carbon and silicon atoms, which the shops offer as a bit shinier and yet a lot cheaper alternative to real diamond.

Accepting the classification of these jewels as diamond and moissanite, we are happily ignorant of the bonding defects between their atoms. However, it's not helpful to ignore the bonding defects between the atoms in our genes. Some of these defects result in gene mutations, possibly with dramatic consequences. On the negative side, mutations can cause disorders and lead to diseases, such as cancers. On the positive side are small genetic differences, which would not exist without gene mutations. Can you imagine a world where all humans are clones of Adam and Eve? The genetic difference between us—the humans—and chimpanzees is less than two percent, but we cherish it. The genetic difference between you, us, and Adolf Hitler is less than half a percent, but it makes a big difference.

The laws of physics and chemistry ignore atomic fluctuations but, analogously to crystal defects, the gene mutations also originate from these fluctuations. The lack of this insight is the gap between the rigid laws in exact sciences and the flexibility of biological evolution, cognition, and creativity. This is the intellectual gap we want to bridge with knowledge that will support our discussion at the intelligence level and, subsequently, at the emotional-intelligence level.

You will no longer have confidence in the laws of physics when you bridge this gap, but you should not worry about that because, ironically, the "eternal" laws of physics also evolve. Believing the laws of physics, as they existed in 1878, Philipp von Jolly advised Max Planck not to go into physics, justifying his advice with the following words: "... in this field, almost everything is already discovered, and all that remains is to fill a few unimportant holes." [16]

Luckily, Planck, who won the Nobel Prize for Physics in 1918, did not listen to his teacher and subsequently became one of the pioneers of quantum mechanics—the fundamental theory of the properties and behavior of small particles, such as molecules, atoms, electrons, and photons (the light particles).

Use math for calculations, but stay away from its infectious perfection.

Physicists have settled on a unique mathematical formalism of quantum mechanics, but they offer more than a dozen interpretations how this math formalism corresponds to reality. That is why the following joke about a student sitting for a physics exam is possible:

> The student: "Professor, these questions are from the last year's exam!"
>
> The professor: "It does not matter, the answers are different."

This joke is also possible for math exams. The following question from a third-grade math quiz in a New York school illustrates the unexpected problem:

> Use the repeated addition strategy to solve: 5x3.[17]

The repeated addition strategy refers to adding the same number again and again to find the answer to a multiplication problem. The teacher marked down a student who answered 5+5+5=15 and wrote the correct answer as 3+3+3+3+3=15. However, the teacher's rule could change and the correct answer could become 5+5+5=15. That is why the nerds began debating the teacher's action when a copy of the marked paper appeared on the internet. According to some, the teacher was correct because 5x3 means 5 groups of 3; for example, 5 groups of 3 apples, or 5 spoons of 3 milliliters of medicine. According to another group, the student was correct because 5x3 means that 5 is repeated 3 times; for example, a 5-milliliter spoon of medicine is taken 3 times. A third group thought that the student was correct because, according to the math law of commutation, 5x3=3x5. But this group could not provide an example. They could not say that 3 milliliters of medicine taken 5 times a day is the same as 5 milliliters of medicine taken 3 times a day. The perfect mathematical symmetry between 5x3 and 3x5 does not represent reality. This teacher might have been onto something by not accepting that 5x3 is the same as 3x5. However, the teacher's rule remains abstract without the physical units and the real meaning of the numbers "3" and "5".

The following joke illustrates that omitted physical units is not the only problem with math abstractions:

> A mathematician wants to test the intelligence of a scientist and an engineer. The mathematician asks them to decide whether they would play a hypothetical game with the following rules: "Imagine you are competing for a golden coin, which is placed 100 meters away from you. You can run, but you must stop when the first runner reaches the half mark at 50 meters. Then, I'd fire the starting gun again, and you could race again until a runner reaches the next half mark, which is 25 meters away from the coin. And so on."

> The scientist fires his answer: "Of course I wouldn't play. The distance from the 100-meter mark would be halved after each run, but the number of runs needed to drop the distance to zero is *infinite*."

> However, the engineer says he would play, prompting the mathematician to announce his mocking judgment: "You don't get it, do you?"

> The engineer is amused: "Where is the problem? After the first run, I am 50 meters away; after the second run, the distance is 25 meters; after the third run, it is 12.5 meters; ...after the 8th run, it drops to 39 centimeters. I can grab the coin from there."

These are all smart people, but their intelligence relates to different values. For the mathematician and the scientist, the perfection of mathematics is the central value, because they need it for the mathematical proofs of absolute laws. Accordingly, the mathematician and the scientist consider the *perfect* zero distance as the final step in this game. For the engineer, the purpose of mathematics is to perform useful calculations—no more, no less.

Accept that chance can trigger unpredictable cause-and-effect chains.

Climate models is an example of math equations whose purpose is to provide us with quantified predictions. Many businesses, governments, and other people use these predictions to make critical decisions.

Climate models incorporate many possible causes, such as greenhouse gas emissions and changes in sunspots. One of the causes for greenhouse emissions is human activities, but we will leave for later the discussion about predictability of human actions. Regarding the changes in sunspots, science tells us that the cause is changes in the sun's magnetic field. But what causes the changes in the sun's magnetic field?

One possibility is random fluctuations of the particles creating the magnetic field, which implies that the first events in this cause-and-effect chain occur purely by chance. It means that we cannot predict—not even in principle—specific changes in the sun's magnetic field and, hence, we cannot predict the climate changes due to this factor. The ignorance in the sense that something cannot be known is different from the ignorance in the sense that we simply don't know something.

We can't blame you if you find it difficult to accept that random events initiate cause-and-effect chains. The belief that absolutely nothing can happen without a cause is common; it is also the starting point for reasoning and arguments by most scientists. Philosophers describe this idea by the word "determinism." In the example of sunspots and the sun's magnetic field, determinism implies that *something* had to cause the changes in the sun's magnetic field, even if we don't know what. However, this just shifts the question of the initial cause a step back. The idea that the cause for changes in the sun's magnetic field has to be something that we don't know, which in turn is caused by something else, leads to an infinite cause-and-effect chain.

Therefore, *the cause-and-effect chains are either infinite or they begin with random events*. Einstein summarized these two alternatives in a letter to Max Born by the following words:

> You believe in the God who plays dice, and I in complete law and order in a world which objectively exists...[18]

We can say that Einstein's complete law and order is consistent with the idea of infinite cause-and-effect chains, but it is inconsistent with the theory of big bang. If there was nothing before the big bang, then there was nothing to cause it, which means that the big bang had to be an unprovoked random event. You may wish to disregard this issue as a purely philosophical problem, but what is important here is the inconsistency of the physicists professing both determinism and the big-bang theory. Why would you ignore this inconsistency to adopt their belief that causeless events cannot happen?

Do not forget that chance has two faces: bad luck and good luck.

In terms of scientific predictions, chance is bad luck because it scatters the experimental data around a theoretical expectation. We are taught to attribute this scattering to experimental errors, but this leads to bad decisions when a rigid theory turns out to be more precise than reality. In real life, the chance that gene mutations will initiate cancerous cells is also bad luck. Our immune system removes newly formed cancerous cells, but it is not perfect and its effectiveness tends to drop as we age, especially in the light of bad lifestyle choices. The implication is that we can minimize the impact of bad luck by creating a healthier environment for the mechanisms in our bodies. The business implication is that creating a healthy working environment is the best defense against inevitable instances of bad luck.

However, there is also good luck in real life. A lottery win is an example of good luck, which also conveys an important warning—good luck is too rare to be squandered. Putting aside the extreme examples of good and bad luck, it is fair to say that instances of bad luck are far more frequent. However, we can utilize a rare instance of good luck to make a much bigger difference.

An example of a big difference is the development of the first marketable incandescent lamp by Thomas Alva Edison. Incandescent lamps were demonstrated well before Edison's development and Edison was able to replicate the previous results when he started his development. But these were short-lived lamps and Edison did not try to build a business with them. He concluded that a lamp would have to last longer than 1,000 hours to be accepted by the potential customers.

Thinking that the lamp filaments were the cause for the short lifetimes, Edison undertook trials of different materials. The first attempt was a failure. The second guess was also a failure. He continued. The tenth filament material also failed. At this stage, most people would've interpreted these experimental results as the certainty of continued failures if the search for better filaments was to continue. Short of giving up, the only hope would've been to try something else.

This logic would've been right if the actual lifetimes were

something like 600 hours for the first filament, 603 hours for the second, 599 for the third, 601 for the fourth, and so on. No doubt, Edison would have also concluded that the changes in filament materials didn't make a significant difference. However, he continued his search, and he did it because there was a significant uncertainty about the achievable lifetime. Let's say that the lifetime was 600 hours with the first filament, 500 hours with the second, 800 with the third, 550 with the fourth, and so on. All these times are shorter than the desired 1,000 hours. They are all failures. However, the differences between these times are quite large. If we focus on these differences, rather than ignore them, we can see that the lifetimes of untested materials would be highly uncertain. We should expect much shorter lifetimes, and most likely quite frequently, but we are also right to expect a much longer lifetime and perhaps even longer than 1,000 hours.

To benefit from this uncertainty of lifetimes, Edison didn't care about the number of failures. He only needed one successful material, which he could use in his commercial incandescent lamp. With real data about the variation of measured lifetimes, and with some math, it's possible to estimate the number of future trials that would be needed for eventual success. Even if this number is in the thousands, the benefit of commercial light bulb would be an excellent payoff for the investment into unsuccessful trials. That's why Edison persisted through more than 6,000 filament materials and classified each of them as bad luck, but with two positive implications:

1. The persistent decisions not to build a business with any of the short-lived lamps—more than 6,000 consecutive decisions—saved valuable resources and time to enable him to keep trying new filaments.

2. Classifying the persistent failures as bad luck, he focused on the possibility that a future trial could

succeed. Instead of overgeneralizing the past failures, Edison was guided by the large uncertainty about the lifetimes in future trials, which he could deduce from the large variations of already tried materials. In other words, there was no certainty to rule out the possibility that a new filament material would work.

Eventually, the good luck turned up and Edison did not squander it. He built a successful business.

Ignore the authority of experts if they put reason ahead of facts.

Most scientists dismiss the type of knowledge that helped Edison develop the marketable incandescent lamp. They despise the idea of random trials, rejecting physicist Max Born's view that chance is a more fundamental concept than causality. People prefer Einstein's belief in complete law and order and they even consider him as one of the smartest persons of all time. Einstein earned this fame when he formulated links between space and time, between rest energy and mass, and many other links by precise mathematical equations, whereas nobody before him could see these links.

In contrast to Einstein's fame, very few people have heard of Agostino Bassi—the first person to demonstrate experimentally the link between germs and disease. He established this link at the time when people did not know about the existence of living organisms that are invisible without magnification. Many factors could be behind people's preference for Einstein's links, but one of them is the appeal of mathematical precision, which asserts the ultimate triumph of reason.

Einstein lived with his true belief in reason, but most of us will be much safer to live with Bassi's motto:

When Fact speaks Reason is silent, because Reason is the child of Fact, not Fact the child of Reason.[19]

At the business level, an example of belief in reason is the idea that developing proper processes is the way of preventing unexpected problems. Yet, the prevailing fact is that unpredictable events are unavoidable and the best way to prepare for the instances of both bad and good luck is to focus on the work environment.

Do not believe that the law of large numbers removes uncertainty.

Opposite to Bassi's motto, when mathematical reason speaks in science, the fact about random events is silent. For example, when scientists speak about models for climate predictions, they are silent about random weather events. Their method is to average the effects of many small weather events by the definition of non-random climate. This approach is an example of "the law of large numbers," which dates back to the work of Swiss mathematician Jakob Bernoulli in 1713. He was analyzing games of chance while trying to develop a probability theory. So, if you're gambling and the outcome is either a win or a loss, is it possible to predict whether you will win or lose after a large number of trials?

In theory, you have a one-in-two chance of choosing the actual outcome in a coin toss—heads or tails. In reality, we all know that it's possible to do a coin toss and have either heads or tails come up twice in a row. Bernoulli showed that if you keep tossing, when you exceed 1,000 tosses, the outcome will be pretty close to half heads and half tails.

A store manager would be relying on the law of large numbers in planning that a certain product will sell at a relatively stable rate, even though the purchase decisions of individual customers are unpredictable. Yet, the law of large numbers won't make the purchase rate more stable. If it did, we wouldn't have something known as the "gambler's fallacy." Going back to the coin toss, if you think that four tosses yielding a "tails" outcome increase your chance of getting a "heads" outcome on the fifth toss, you are subscribing to the gambler's fallacy. Each toss is an independent event unaffected by what came before it.

As a gambler—or a business professional planning the number of deals your company could sign in the year ahead—you should know that Bernoulli's result is about the mathematical *average* of wins and not about the actual wins and losses in reality. The resources of your company may be adequate for—on average—a deal every two months, but the reality of successive failures to close deals, like the gambler's unfortunate series of four "tails," might be enough to doom your business. On the other hand, if your company accepts a cluster of several deals in a single week, a lack of resources might also turn into a serious problem.

The law of large numbers helps us to establish what fraction of many trials will be successful, but it does not remove the real effects of randomness.

Be aware that comparisons of percentages can hide both large differences and large similarities.

Whatever phrase we use to quantify a fraction—one in two, or 50 percent, or a half—this concept is a mathematical generalization that could mean different things to different people. Here is an example of a smart girl who comes across the following question as she is doing her homework: "You have ten apples. How many apples will you have after you give a half to your brother?" "Nine and a half" is the girl's answer! She is correct because the ratio stated as "a half" doesn't specify that the divisor is ten apples.

Not knowing the value of the divisor in ratios between large numbers can trick us into overgeneralizations. For example, the human genome is a concept that ignores the genetic differences between individual humans because the difference is less than half a percent. Many experts extend this general-ization further by their implicit assumption that all human bodies share the same biological mechanisms. Based on this generalization, your doctor is able to compare your cholesterol level to the average number calculated from a large group of healthy people.

But we are not all identical and your body may not respond according to a doctor's expectation based on compar-isons to an average patient. The relative genetic difference of 0.5 percent corresponds to the absolute difference of about one billion atoms and, consequently, corresponds to signif-icant functional differences. Still, this does not negate the fact that the similarity between individual genomes is even larger—about 200 billion atoms.

In contrast, the larger 8.3-percent mass difference between carbon-12 and carbon-13 atoms corresponds to a single neutron. Apart from this mass difference, the single neutron does not create a significant difference in the functionalities of these atoms. We can see that, because of the large number of genes, human genomes are both more similar and more differ-ent in comparison to the similarities and differences between the two carbon isotopes. The comparison between 0.5 percent and 8.3 percent hides this effect. Moreover, it implies that the difference between genomes is negligible in comparison to the difference between isotopes, which is another misleading effect of "the law of large numbers."

In summary, you should not believe mathematical transformations and scientific theories that overgeneralize observed similarities—they are inconsistent with the concepts of tolerance, risk, and a degree of uncertainty. Typical red flags are statements that something is correct because it is proved mathematically and that something either has to happen or cannot happen because of the laws of physics. The law of large numbers is not a reason to believe in the absence of macroscopic randomness. Random events will affect our lives. Awareness that everything originates from random events is necessary to avoid the overgeneralization traps of true beliefs. Now we will expand this awareness and put it to work.

2

No Process Can Avoid Unpredictable Events

To reveal what they fear the most about the future, some politicians quote the following words attributed to Harold Macmillan, the British Prime Minister from 1957 to 1963: "Events, dear boy. Events."[20]

It's a puzzling quote. From one point of view, it reflects wisdom—instead of creating false expectations, it concedes that unexpected events can disrupt even the best planned process. We all know how the biggest economic event in our lifetimes—due to the coronavirus pandemic in 2020—disrupted almost every industry and every government in the world. Much smaller events are far more frequent, but they also can be quite disruptive.

From another point of view, Macmillan's words look like a preemptive excuse for inadequate processes and poor control of events. Beyond any cynicism, the logic here is that events result from processes—they don't just happen out of nowhere. This logic stems from engineers' ability to control production processes, and it underpins the management of business processes.

The events we observe in everyday life do result from processes. In the example of coronavirus pandemic, numerous events of business shutdowns resulted from the process of virus spreading around the world. However, this transmission process started with a single event—the appearance of the very first specimen of this new virus. That's why people debate whether this event was preventable. Obviously, it would've been much better if that event did not occur, rather than trying to stop the transmission process once it started. The debate about the cause of the very first specimen is about the process that lead to this event. It was either a process of natural evolution, or—if the event occurred in a lab—it was a consequence of someone's thinking process. However, neither evolution nor thinking are the first triggers in this process-and-event chain. For example, any thinking process consists of neuron-firing events, which in turn result from ion-flow processes.

Process-and-event chains are like the chicken-and-egg dilemma. In fact, this is the most fundamental chicken-and-egg dilemma, where the actual question is: Which comes first, an event or a process?

We are taking you to a deep intellectual dive with this somewhat philosophical question, but we are doing it to show why neither business managers nor technical people should focus solely on their processes. The fundamental problem is our human intuition that any change in nature is fundamentally continuous. Unsurprisingly, this is also a core scientific premise. With this intuition and premise, Gottfried Leibniz and Isaac Newton invented the mathematics of continuous change, called calculus, and people have used it to model processes from the fundamental physics to economics. Famous examples of these equations include Solow–Swan's model of economic growth, Black–Scholes's model for pricing of options, the predator—prey equations in biology, Newton's laws in mechanics, Maxwell's equations of electrodynamics, Einstein's field equations, and Schrödinger's equation in quantum mechanics.

This widespread use of calculus conceals a problem with its premise. The problem is that the fundamental concept of continuous change is different from reality. You need to see this difference. It will challenge your trust in processes, and it may seem at times as a philosophical desire to open a can of worms. However, we want you to see the root of all dangers and all opportunities. Then, we will have a solid ground to talk about the best ways to avoid dangers and to utilize opportunities.

You don't need to buy a "pig in a poke" if calculus is the "poke." (*For younger readers, a "poke" is a bag, so a pig in a poke is a concealed pig, meaning you don't know what you're getting.*)

In December 2018, the US Government enacted the National Quantum Initiative Act without any real debate. They simply trusted the experts warning them about grave security implications if US fell behind China and behind the European Union in the areas of quantum computing and communications. The Act authorized $1.2 billion to be invested in quantum information science over the next ten years, which is a similar funding level to the quantum master plan developed by the European Union. Still, this dwarfs Chinese investment of $10 billion to build National Laboratory for Quantum Information Sciences in Hefei, the home city of the Chinese "father of quantum"—Dr. Pan Jianwei. According to Chinese media, President Xi Jinping takes personal interest in Pan's work and occasionally visits his labs. During New

Year's address in January 2018, the President praised Chinese progress in quantum computing as he stressed the strategic importance of quantum technologies.

All these governments are reacting to repeated warning that quantum computers have the potential to break the strongest forms of encryption, which is protecting the deepest financial and military secrets. It's a concerted claim by scientists, and it spells both serious dangers and tantalizing opportunities in the escalating information war. Interestingly, scientists also claim that a unique quantum phenomenon could enable an unbreakable level of security by a new form of communication.

Taking these predictions seriously, governments have to make decisions in the absence of functional prototypes of such world-changing quantum systems. We don't know how President Xi makes this kind of decisions, but it's possible that he simply took for granted what scientists told him. However, we do know about an attempt by the Canadian Prime Minister Justin Trudeau, to gain some understanding of quantum theory. In April 2016, he visited the Perimeter Institute for Theoretical Physics in Waterloo, Ontario, to announce funding of $50 million for their research. During the visit, he made an effort to grasp the crux of quantum computing, and then volunteered the following succinct explanation to the attending journalists:

> A regular computer bit is either a 1 or a 0—on or off. A quantum state can be much more complex than that because as we know, things can be both particle and wave at the same time and the uncertainty around quantum states allows us to encode more information into a much smaller computer. So that's what's exciting about quantum computing.[21]

We all know that politicians sometimes like to be both *for* and *against* something at the same time. With this in mind, the Prime Minister's resonance with the analogous idea of things being both particle and wave at the same time makes some sense. When politicians milk the uncertainty to encode both *yes* and *no* options in the same answer, they implement his statement that uncertainty "allows us to encode more information."

Apart from that, you can bet Trudeau's sentences didn't make sense to the attending journalists. But, it didn't really matter. He appeared as the smartest person in the room, and his apparently erudite explanation sparked intense media coverage from around the world.

Seemingly jealous of the popularity of Prime Minister's explanation, some scientists denigrated it as incorrect. Well, if that is so, here is a description from the horse's mouth— Dr. Pan's sentences quoted in a serious article in *The Washington Post*:

> As we all know, in our everyday life, a cat can only either be in an alive or dead state, but a cat in the quantum world can be in a coherent superposition of alive and dead states.[22]

Wow! A respected scientist is taken seriously and awarded billions of dollars in funding to pursue the idea of quantum cats in combined dead-and-alive states!

Scientists frequently use this bizarre description because it relates to Erwin Schrödinger—one of the pioneers of quantum theory and the physicist whose equation has been accepted as the mathematical formalism of quantum mechanics. This equation combines mutually exclusive states, in analogy with a politician's sentence stating that both *yes* and *no* options exist. Another analogy is the statement that both *heads* and *tails* are possible outcomes of a coin flip. There is nothing wrong if a sentence combines heads as the winning option and tails as the losing option. However, to see how physicists think, ignore the reality that the winning heads and the losing tails are simply two possible outcomes. Instead, consider that a mathematical combination of heads and tails is a single and a direct representation of reality. This is how physicists think when they consider the mathematical combination of mutually exclusive states as real. It's not either a win or a loss. The cat is not either dead or alive; it's both dead and alive, according to the equation combining these states.

Schrödinger ultimately abandoned quantum mechanics, explaining his decision by the following words: "I do not like it, and I'm sorry I ever had anything to do with it."[23] Of course, we also have the option of turning our heads away. We can ignore the warning that the future information wars will be won or lost in the quantum world. We don't really need to bang our heads against this specific wall. That way, we would leave it to governments to deal with these scientists and to fund these projects as an insurance policy. However, this example has a general implication.

Ask yourself whether you'd extend this kind of insurance purchasing to your own decisions. How many times are you prepared to buy snake oil because you feel stupid to ask questions? And just because this quantum business is so much beyond common sense, it's an excellent example to show that you don't need to be an expert to find a useful question. In this example, you wouldn't be stupid to ask the scientists why they believe in what they themselves describe as bizarre phenomena.

The answer you will hear is that the weird interpretations of quantum theory don't really matter. Apparently, they don't, and the supposedly profound reason is this: The experts don't need these interpretations because they rely on experimental proofs of Schrödinger's equation when they use it.

We are expected to take this kind of answer for granted. If we dare to be skeptical about the reliance on math, we are likely to provoke patronizing reactions. That's because experimentally proven math governs the scientific world. It is not only the calculus in Schrödinger's equation, and not only the calculus for process modeling. The reliance on experimentally proven math is a big deal. For example, at the fringe of math spectrum, statistical theorems rule the science behind the legal approvals of drugs and vaccines. We may have doubts about some of these approvals, but the experts expect us to lay down our arms when facing an argument based on experimentally proven math.

During the coronavirus pandemic in 2020, authorities followed selected experts and used mathematics to justify unprecedented business shutdowns and to persuade people to lock themselves at home. The Governor of New York, Andrew Cuomo, said: "We have a model, a projection, and that's what we follow." Within two months, he changed his mind. He shocked a lot of political observers by his admission that it was wrong to follow model projections.

Discussing this admission, Seth Cohen, a leadership-strategy contributor to *Forbes*, depicted Cuomo's change of heart as an important example of reflective leadership. The following sentence summarizes Cohen's reasoning: "Yes, in the early days of this pandemic many of us have made mistakes—and even failed—but learning from our mistakes quickly could be our greatest success of all."[24]

We agree. However, to learn quickly also means that people should stop repeating the same mistakes. It's even better to learn from the failures of others. In this specific case of math models, the key thing to learn is why experimental proofs don't turn these models into reliable truths.

This may seem as a hard question to crack. In one or another way, Sima has been in the business of experimental data and modeling from graduation in 1982. With time, he learned why *evidence-based models* are not necessarily *reliable models*, and that many decision makers are unaware of this difference when they use evidence-based models. Yet, grasping this important difference is not hard. The problem is our education—we learn about successful applications of math and scientific models, but we don't learn why failures happen. When Governor Cuomo decided to follow the models, he wasn't even aware how wrong they could be. That's unhelpful, so we offer you here an opportunity to learn *why* failures of math and proven science are unavoidable.

The following insight is the first step in this learning process: You can sense that an expert may be selling "a pig in a poke" even if you don't have a clue about the related math and science.

The magic of quantum physics is an excellent example of experts selling a pig in a poke. In October 2019, most TV stations, newspapers, and magazines reported Google's claim that their quantum computer performed calculations no ordinary computer could complete. According to Google, this was the first demonstration of the so-called "quantum supremacy," and it was a big news. However, the reporters had to pass this news without the ability to verify it. Here is why. When the experts use a quantum computer, they go through math theorems and assumptions. This is very different from your ordinary use of smart phones and real computers. If you don't want to see any symbols or obscure numbers, you cannot see the operation of a quantum computer. Non-removable math wraps the claimed quantum advantage. Some reporters are smart enough to see this point, but they missed it. Perhaps the reason was their belief that Google's experts were presenting a truth. Yet, the reality is this: If no one can see the quantum pig in the math poke, what we have is no more than interpretations.

With this, we are contradicting the experts' claim that interpretations don't matter when they use experimentally proven equations. So how do we go about interpreting experimental facts?

Use the mathematical models of any process only as approximations.

After World War II, the president of Toyota Motor Company decided to compete with the American car makers. The core of his strategy was to eliminate waste by an approach that was initially known as the *Toyota Production System*. This production system was later popularized as *lean* manufacturing and *lean* consumption.[25,26] In theory, any inventory of raw materials, parts, or finished products results in wasted time, resources, and materials. In the ideal implementation of the lean system, all needed parts should arrive at the factory *just in time* to be assembled straight away, and the factory should deliver the finished product *just in time* to a waiting customer. The ideal aims are zero waiting time, zero inventory, reduced batch sizes, and reduced process times by delivering "the right things, to the right place, at the right time, in the right quantity to achieve perfect work flow."[27]

The concept of "perfect flow" is the ideal scenario, which is embodied by calculus-based process modeling. Ideal aims, such as zero waiting time and zero inventory in the lean system, are the optimum solutions of these models. Clearly, the phrase "to achieve perfect workflow" describes an aspirational aim that no one can achieve. The intention of such aspirational aims is to guide continuous improvements toward perfection. However, we all know that zero waiting time and zero inventory are not the optimum solutions in reality. The concept of continuous improvement toward the perfect flow hides a limit, which doesn't exist in the math of continuous change, but it does exist in reality.

In the first months of 2020, Japan's car manufacturing had to stop. The Chinese Government enacted business lockdowns to prevent uncontrolled spread of the coronavirus, and the supply of necessary parts from China stopped. With a focus on the aspirational aim of perfect flow, managers couldn't realize how close their lean manufacturing was to an abyss. Yet, just a tiny virus was able to disrupt the continuity and the momentum of such a huge process of supply, manufacturing, and distribution.

It helps to see the limit of continuity, and to understand why truly unpredictable disruptions are possible. To get to these insights, we will use our *lean* example of recommended cost cutting by fabrication of organic sauces on demand. This is our hypothetical and simple fabrication-on-demand example in the Introduction. We will focus on the concepts of purchase and supply rates, because the recommended cost-cutting method boils down to equalizing the purchase and supply rates to avoid both costly oversupply and disruptive undersupply.

If a given supermarket sells 6,000 jars of this sauce over the period of one year, a possible calculation of the purchase rate could be 6,000/12=500 jars per month. However, this is only the *average* purchase rate, which does not show that the supermarket may need only 200 jars in June and as many as 800 jars in December. The concept of average purchase rate is not sufficiently precise to enable the needed equalizing of purchase and supply rates. But what is the precise purchase rate?

For a weekly supply of sauces to this supermarket, we could calculate the purchase rate using a week as the relevant time interval. However, this is still an average rate. We may wish to know how the precise rate changes during the day, so that the purchase data can account for different profiles of customers shopping during middays and during evenings. Here, we reached a continuity limit: If we calculate the purchase rate for every minute during the day, the data will no longer reflect a purchasing *process* but rather purchasing *events*—mostly zero and occasionally one jar per minute.

So, we see that purchasing processes consist of purchasing events, but this example doesn't rule out the possibility that purchase decisions could be predictable. Customer profiling is about classifying purchasing decisions, which implies some regularity and, ultimately, predictability. After all, these decisions result from neural processes that could be—at least in principle—predictable. Neuroscience does regard decision making as a continuous cognitive process. However, as we already mentioned, cognitive processes consist of neuron-firing events, which in turn result from processes of ion flow into and out of neurons. The flow of ions creates electrical signals that neuroscientists can measure by placing electrodes on your head. For a decision process that takes a second or so, the neuroscientist would like to see changes in the electrical signals within tiny fractions of the second. At this point, it's insightful to think about the best possible precision to ensure that no change in a signal is missed.

Scientists and engineers model the rate of ion flow by adopting Leibniz and Newton's concept of an *infinitely small* increment of time. That way, no change in a signal can be missed because the signal cannot jump between two instants of time that are inseparably close to each other; in other words, the corresponding change in this continuous signal is also infinitely small. The calculus name for the idea of an infinitely small change is *infinitesimal*, which is the key concept in the mathematics of absolutely continuous processes.

However, the infinitesimal—the key calculus concept—is so small that it doesn't exist in the reality of whole units, such as ions and jars. The rate of ion flow, which creates the neural signals, is analogous to the rate at which shoppers buy sauce jars. Assume that six sauce jars are purchased individually over the period of sixty minutes. The purchase rate expressed as 6/60=0.1 purchases per minute may be a useful mathematical abstraction for some calculations, but it certainly doesn't mean that the shop could be selling fractions of sauce jars. The absolute precision of calculus is inaccurate because its key concept—the infinitesimal—is smaller than the whole units in reality.

To avoid fractions, we can say that a purchase is made every ten minutes. However, this is still different from reality because the jars will not be taken off the shelves at regular ten-minute intervals. Instead, the actual observed times between two purchasing events could be something like 8, 21, 9, and 11, all in the unit of minutes. Analogous fluctuations in time intervals exist between the ions entering a neuron, except the unit would be picoseconds. These random fluctuations are significant and experimentally-observed features of reality.

This insight gives us more than we expected from the answer to the question whether an event or a process comes first: *Not only do events come first, but they also occur with a degree of randomness.*

Scientists continue to dig deeper to find a process that will kill the observed randomness, but no luck. All process-and-event chains begin with random events, and that's what enables the evolution of new things; that's what makes the future different from the past. We will end here our deep philosophical dive and turn our attention to the implications of this insight. These implications exist because the randomness of fundamental events rolls over to our decision processes. It happens when you do something that you usually don't do and all you can say is "I don't know why I did that." It also happens in your light-bulb moments, when you get a new idea from nowhere.

The implication for the streamlined fabrication-on-demand

process is that the fundamental randomness negates the possibility of equalizing purchase and supply rates.

No process in nature can be as predictable as implied by its calculus-based models. This contrasts the view of most scientists who see some calculus equations as autonomous laws of nature that humans merely discovered. However, showing why continuous equations don't match the reality of discrete units and events—an insight that Sima also presented to the readers of *Skeptic* magazine[28]—we have to conclude that scientists invented the laws of nature. The equations formulating these laws are idealized approximations, which are no more than useful calculation tools and we shouldn't overgeneralize their implications.

Respect the arrow of time.

In contrast to the concept of process continuity, the defining feature of repeatable events is that they are clearly distinguishable and countable units. For example, neuron-firing events are distinguishable because the neurons reach their rest condition before firing again; in other words, there is an eventless interval between two consecutive firing events.

The time gap between consecutive events sets the arrow of time from the preceding to the subsequent event. With the set arrow of time, events are fundamentally irreversible. When your neurons fire to get you to say or do something, these actions become irreversible.

This should be unremarkable, except it contradicts the logic of greatest experts in exact sciences whose impact in broader society is considerable. For example, most news outlets reported Stephen Hawking's views when his latest book, *Brief Answers to the Big Questions*[29], was published soon after his death. The title of *Forbes*'s post on October 16, 2018, is illustrative: "Stephen Hawking believed time travel was more likely than the existence of God."[30] Acknowledging that "one has to be careful not to be labelled a crank," Hawking saw traveling back in time as "a very serious question" and the reason was that Einstein's theory of general relativity "can permit time travel." The book publicized his concern that "if one made a research grant application to work on time travel it would be dismissed immediately."

In spite of such a broad interest in Hawking's way of thinking, government agencies indeed don't fund grant applications aimed at investigating the "very serious question" of time travel. We teach our children and students that anything can happen if they dream big enough, so we shouldn't be surprised if some of them get excited about building a time-travelling rocket. After all, the next generation should go a step further and outdo Elon Musk's rockets. However, no business development could happen until someone demonstrates a positive answer to Hawking's question about traveling back in time. The practical question then is why government agencies don't fund this type of projects, even though they are paying universities to teach the laws of physics in accordance with Hawking's way of thinking.

This practical question goes beyond the extreme example of time travel. In its more general form, the question is why our society celebrates and teaches the logic of Newton, Einstein, and Hawking's science if, in reality, the responsible people in power make decisions based on contradicting intuition.

Take climate science as an example. In December 2015, representatives from 195 nations around the world and from the European Union met near Paris and negotiated an agreement for mitigation of greenhouse-gas emissions, known as the Paris Agreement. It seemed that most of these representatives had adopted the logic of exact sciences, which they demonstrated by repeated use of phrases such as "climate science is settled." Yet, the final agreement unveils their startling reluctance to make decisions according to the "settled science." The words of Barak Obama, the US President at the time, convey this reluctance: "Now, the Paris Agreement alone will not solve the climate crisis. Even if we meet every target embodied in the agreement, we'll only get to part of where we need to go".[31] The acceptance that climate science traced the path "where we need to go" was contradicted by the decision-makers' reluctance to go beyond not only non-compulsory targets but also targets that fell short of the accepted science. Why this contradiction? You might think of these people as politicians who don't care about the long-term impact of their decisions, but they do care about the views of their voters.

The answer we offer in this chapter is this: In both cases, the time travel and climate change, the intuition of the decision makers is correct. However, they are unable to explain the discrepancy between their decisions and the related science. They don't know why science creates counter-intuitive implications that the past can be changed by traveling back in time, whereas the future of climate change is certain. And, of course, it's always a problem when a decision maker cannot provide a more convincing justification than hand-waving or gut feeling.

We need to be able to disregard confidently any science that messes around with the arrow of time by implying that the future is certain whereas the past could be changed. These contradictory interpretations are possible because scientists have formulated the laws of physics by continuous equations, which rigidly link the past and the future. In Leibniz and Newton's calculus, these rigid links ignore the arrow of time with the concept of infinitely small changes—the infinitesimals—which do not exist in the real world of whole units. That's why the laws of science are no more than useful approximations, with the absolute continuity as the key idealized feature.

In reality, random events separate the uncertain future from the determined past. Probabilities of events range from very high to very low, but the uncertainty associated with any probability relates only to future events. Once an event occurs, the outcome becomes certain and it no longer matters whether its probability for occurrence was high or low. A coin toss is a simple example: the uncertainty and the chance of one in two is in the future; once the coin drops, the outcome becomes certain.

Always check the specific interpretation of experimental data.

Seeing that the uncertain future is different from the determined past, we have to be careful about the common claims about proven laws, proven methods, proven steps, proven track record, and so on. When someone claims proven track record from the past, you shouldn't hear "proven success in the future." The certainty of facts is in the past, not in the future. Whatever the proven facts are, *we are interpreting these facts as soon as we make a judgment about their impact in the future.*

Take a lottery win as an extreme example. After a draw, the correct choice of the winning numbers is "experimentally proven." The win becomes a fact from the past with a significant impact on the winner's future, who suddenly becomes a financial outlier. Of course, lottery win is a fact that's easy to interpret as pure luck, meaning that the winner has no real expertise and the success is unlikely to happen again in the future. The interpretation of business outliers is trickier. Could you become as rich as Bill Gates without luck?

According to Malcolm Gladwell, the author of *Outliers: The Story of Success*,[32] the element of extraordinary luck is a part of any extraordinary success. He explains that inherited talent and hard work are necessary but not sufficient conditions for someone to succeed well beyond many others and to appear as an outlier. Analogously to the way a winning lottery ticket creates an outlier, a rare luck separates the outliers from others who are just as talented and work just as hard. These rare events are what Taleb calls "black swans" in his books,[33] as he exposes the illusion that extraordinary wins by some people provide the empirical evidence of their extraordinary expertise.

On the flip side, a failure doesn't necessarily prove a lack of expertise and it doesn't negate future successes.

Both successes and failures are undeniable facts from the past, but interpretations of these facts can be very different. It is a fact when a company posts an increased profit. The Board of the company may interpret this fact as the key evidence of effective leadership by their CEO and, consequently, may decide to reward the leader with a huge bonus. However, others may attribute the improved profit to unpredictable improvements in the market conditions.

A technical example is the historic fact that a team of an engineer and a physicists, John Bardeen and Walter Brattain, observed amplification of electronic signals on December 15, 1947, while experimenting with solid-state materials at Bell Laboratories in New Jersey. According to one interpretation, this was the accidental invention of the first transistor—the device that initiated the digital revolution. Bardeen and Brattain's group leader, William Shockley, was managing the experiments with a different device concept in mind, hence the interpretation that the invention of the unknown transistor was accidental. According to another interpretation, the invention of the transistor was inevitable because Shockley's concept set up the right experiments. The Nobel-prize committee adopted the second interpretation and recognized Shockley's contribution when they awarded the 1956 prize for the invention of the transistor not only to Bardeen and Brattain but also to Shockley. Yet, the recognized track record of these three experts did not continue during the subsequent commercialization of their invention, which happened without them.

As a different and more recent example, it's a fact that the Northeast states in United States suffered unusually cold winters in 2018 and 2019. Some people interpret this fact as an evidence against the science of global warming, others interpret it as an evidence in support of some global-warming models, whereas a third group interprets it as no more than weather fluctuations.

We all know the mantra that decisions should be based on facts, but do we make sure to distinguish the certainty of facts from their variable interpretations? Even top managers make silly decisions by not checking specific interpretations of experimental facts. Whether it's economic or climate modeling, the decision makers prefer to receive consistent predictions so that they don't need to deal with different interpretations of the facts. With this aim, their approach is to fund more equipment, more powerful computers, and more people to collect and feed as much data as possible into the best available models.

To test this belief with the example of climate models, we can consider the ideal implementation of this approach by the following thought experiment: Assume we have the data about the state of every atom that impacts the climate. Assume also that somehow we have computers able to memorize all these data and to process them through a giant Schrödinger's equation. This equation is the key because quantum physicists compared it to numerous experimental data and, according to them, it's an experimentally proven fact that atoms obey this fundamental equation.

Yet, even in this ideal scenario, no computer can predict the random atom fluctuations and, therefore, couldn't predict the unusually cold winters in US. In this example, the impression of limitless power of computers and big data is wrong, even though it's aligned with what should be experimentally proven science. The question then is whether a non-expert making funding decisions—not only in governments but also in companies such as Intel, Google, and IBM—could see when science steps beyond reality and turns into fiction.

Yes, a non-expert can do it, and it's not really hard. For any science based on continuous math, all you need is to recall our demonstration that calculus—the mathematics of continuous change—models *continuous processes*. This is important because experimental data are records of *discrete events*. Anyone can see that using experimental events to prove a theoretical process is like comparing countable apples and uncountable juice. And it's not only calculus; all continuous math is analogous to uncountable juice, in contrast to the reality of countable events and objects, including—in principle—the atoms in a cup of juice. Countable events and objects are the reality of our quantum world.

If you ask the experts how they compare their continuous models with discrete experimental data, the answer would be revealing. For example, to enable comparisons between Schrödinger's equation and experimental data, the scientists use a simple mathematical transformation—proposed originally by Max Born—to convert the continuous equations into calculated probabilities for countable events. That's cute, but can you see the stepping from the abstract certainty of continuous math back to random events in reality? The idea of experimentally proven quantum math is an overgeneralization—it ignores the difference between measured events and theoretical processes. With this insight, we can confidently disregard it.

Therefore, we can be absolutely confident that no process can make the future certain. In spite of the opposite implication by the calculus-based laws, we can see why Macmillan's lack of faith in his own processes was realistic thinking. The takeaway lesson from this overarching insight is that, instead of perfecting planning processes, it is smarter to work on establishing the conditions for the best chance to deal with unpredictable events, both favorable and unfavorable.

3

More of the Same Works in Stable Conditions

Leo Tolstoy's *Anna Karenina* begins with the following sentence: "Happy families are all alike; every unhappy family is unhappy in its own way."[34]

In his book, *Guns, Germs and Steel*, Jared Diamond popularized the wisdom of this sentence as the Anna Karenina principle.[35] He generalized Tolstoy's sentence by observing that successful trials—analogously to happy families—are similar to one another because they all possess the same set of essential features. All flying birds are alike because they all have wings to fly, long toes to stand on branches, and beaks to collect food and feed their chicks. There are many ways to depart from one or more of the essential features, but these trials—analogously to unhappy families—are doomed to failure.

Businesspeople quote the Anna Karenina principle to

emphasize that success requires all essential boxes to be ticked. Any significant departure from the steps of a proven process or recipe could lead to a failure. But how do we draw the line between essential and inessential steps?

Happy families are all alike, but quality products are *almost* the same.

Voyager 1 and 2 are twin spacecraft, which NASA launched back in 1977. Some time ago, they both left the Solar system, but their microchips are still processing and sending signals from the space between stars. We can only take our hats off to such reliability of a quality product. These microchips were made by RCA Corporation according to their high-reliability process, which they qualified by the testing prescribed in the governing standard for military and aerospace electronic systems.

The two Voyagers sent impressive images of Saturn when they encountered this planet, one after another, in 1981 and 1982. A year later, large posters with Saturn and its eye-catching rings featured on the walls of the engineering room where Sima worked at the time. This was the Semiconductor Factory in Nis, the city of electronics in former Yugoslavia. The factory had a license for RCA's high-reliability process and Sima's job was to study their documentation and to implement the steps for in-line process control. The factory was making high-reliability microchips for Yugoslav army and the aim was to qualify the fabrication process and equipment by a full compliance with the US military standard.

The team was an enthusiastic bunch of engineers, technicians, and operators, working on a leading high-tech program, and everything was going really well. Performance measurements of test devices and functional microchips were spot on. Final results of months-long reliability testing were awaited with confidence. This was the last milestone ahead of the crucial qualification of the team's process and equipment by a panel of army officers. Continued funding for the program and the group by the army was predicated on the forthcoming qualification.

One morning the program director walked into the engineering room and invited Sima to follow him to his office. Judging by his body language, the director had something important to say. He started with the positive things, expressing his confidence in all the team's measurements and expectations for excellent reliability results. Then he asked few questions about the calibration of microscopes, used to measure micrometer-size features on the microchips (a micrometer is a hundred times smaller than the thickness of an average paper). Sima told him that he didn't have any doubt about the dimensions measured with the microscopes because the electrical results were exactly as expected and that's what ultimately mattered.

The logic seemed simple: If cooks in a pizza shop always set the oven temperature at 450 degrees Fahrenheit and the baked pizzas are always as expected, the heaters and the oven are stable. If a device is used to measure the temperature inside the oven and it always shows 450 degrees Fahrenheit, the measurement device is also stable and correct. In theory, however, that logic was back to front. The measurement device should verify the temperature in the oven, rather than baked pizzas verifying the measurement device.

There was an issue with this back-to-front logic—only on paper, but still an issue. The director explained that he had received a list of specific requirements from the army panel in charge of the qualification process. Among other things, they requested certification of the team's *etalon*—a piece of special glass used to calibrate measurement microscopes. The etalon was to be inspected by what was the best military lab in the country for measurements of small dimensions. At the time, Yugoslavia was making fighter aircraft and it turned out the lab was measuring dimensions in the mechanical parts of aircraft engines. Sima immediately aired his concern that a lab equipped for measurements of mechanical parts may not be able to certify the etalon to sub-micrometer precision.

In analogy with the pizza shop, the problem was neither the baked pizzas nor the actual temperature in the oven, but a request to certify a temperature-measurement device. The problem was analogous to an imminent danger that the pizza shop would have to close for a peculiar reason—the independent lab in charge wouldn't be able to measure temperatures as high as 450 degrees Fahrenheit.

The director acknowledged the issue, but also clearly stated the need for a certification paper for the etalon. Otherwise, the military panel would find it difficult to recommend qualification of the equipment and continued funding for the program. His concluding message was along the lines of the following sentence: I hope you understand that problems my engineers have to solve extend beyond pure technical solutions.

Sima travelled to the military lab and met the engineer in charge. The first question the engineer asked was about the dimension of the "smallest trench" in the microchips. The honest answer was that the smallest feature the team was measuring was a 7.4-micrometer wide metal track. The engineer jumped up from his chair, declaring that there was no way they could certify the etalon with such a precision.

Sima thought about this scenario before the meeting and was prepared for it. The problem at that moment was clear: A qualification rule required certification of the team's etalon, but the only acceptable lab by the army couldn't do it with a meaningful precision. Without army's qualification, the funding for the project would stop. Yet, the performance of the final products was spotless and all electrical measurements were well within the specs. In the pizza analogy, it didn't seem right for a profitable shop to shut its door because it couldn't calibrate its temperature-measurement device. So, it was clear the problem was a kind of inadequately prescribed certification procedure. Sima couldn't solve this problem, but he could try to avoid it.

When the military engineer declared that a micrometer precision was beyond the capability of his lab, Sima whispered that this was not exactly what they needed. After some silence, the engineer sat back in his chair and asked for a written statement of what exactly was needed from them. Sima wrote something to the following effect: "We confirm that the precision of the calibration device used by the Semiconductor Factory is well within the precision of our instruments." The idea was to act obediently and avoid the problem by not saying that the requested inspection was blind.

The engineer read the sentence and took the piece of paper to his bosses. He came back after a while with the key phrases embedded in formal sentences, typed on their letterhead, signed, and stamped with a big round stamp that was more important than a signature in Yugoslavia at the time.

Sima took the letter back and his director was happy. He smiled and said something like: That's what we needed. Job well done! Thank you!

The ultimate happiness came months later with excellent results from the reliability tests. With this and with all the paperwork in order, the criteria for qualification of the high-reliability process and equipment had been satisfied. The final inspection by the army panel was successful, which ensured continued funding for the program. The team couldn't replicate RCA's process exactly as presented in their documentation, but managed to get right everything that mattered for the quality and reliability. Expressing it in the terms of the Anna Karenina principle, Sima's team did not fail because they ticked all essential boxes.

Yet, a question lingers here. Why did RCA documentation have inessential items according to that group's experience? If these items waste resources, shouldn't they be identified and removed?

For high quality, do not just tick the key boxes but strictly follow established recipes.

Not long after Sima paid lip service to RCA's microscope calibration, a senior engineer at the IBM General Technology Division challenged his view about inessential items. The late Charles Stapper was working at the time on mathematical models for yield and reliability management in IBM's microchip fabrication. This was after Sima moved back to University of Nis to complete a Master of Science and then PhD degrees. Among other things, he was also working on modeling of microchip yield. Because the microchips consist of a huge number of tiny features, even a single small defect can render the whole chip faulty. "Yield" is the term for the percentage of functional chips. Charles Stapper was the world leader in yield modeling, so the university invited him to its conference on microelectronics, held in Nis in 1989. He was curious about the modeling approach Sima's group was publishing, and this curiosity outweighed his reluctance to travel to a communist country. In addition to the technical sessions, the conference organized a couple of sightseeing days and Sima spent a lot of time talking to Charles.

At the time, Sima was driving Yugo 45, the most popular car in Yugoslavia, which was also exported to the United States and sold for around $4,000. Adjusted for inflation, this was the cheapest car ever sold in US. Many reviews by car experts described the car as the slowest and the worst car ever imported into the country. This criticism was unfair because they compared the extremely simple engine and basic interior of a $4,000 car to at least three times more expensive vehicles.

When more than 100,000 people in the United States bought their Yugos, they were attracted by the extremely low price. These people accepted the fact that the money they were paying would get them a simple engine, a slow vehicle, and a plain interior. The surprises they didn't like emerged when they had to take the car for frequent repairs and maintenance.

Curious about Yugo 45, Charles asked Sima about his experience and Sima told him that he had to take it back for several repairs during the warranty period. In response, Charles contrasted the image of poor car manufacturing by stating that the yield numbers in the Semiconductor Factory were quite impressive. Sima agreed with this observation, adding that he couldn't understand why Yugoslavia as a country could make high-reliability microchips in one factory and fighter jets in another factory, but couldn't make a basic but reliable car. Charles answered this question.

The first thing Charles said seemed like a change of topic. He said that no one worked on yield modeling in Japan. They did not need it, he said, because their yield was 100 percent. No faulty chips. The tiny killer defects didn't exist. He said Japanese could achieve this by disciplined replication of all steps of the fabrication process. There were no essential and inessential steps and there was no variation in the process condition that was acceptable. Charles said this was far too extreme for IBM and their yields were well below 100 percent.

Then he made a general observation about the people he met in Yugoslavia. He said he saw people considering themselves as smart enough to decide on their own that some rules were inessential and could be disregarded. For the team at the Semiconductor Factory, it was essential to achieve high reliability of microchips, in compliance with the US standard for military and aerospace electronic systems. Because the funding was predicated on the high reliability of these microchips, the engineers tightened the process control and, as a result, the chip yields were also quite high. In contrast, high reliability was not necessary for the car manufacturer. For them, it was essential to deliver cheap cars that the people in Yugoslavia, and even more so in other communist countries of Eastern Europe, could afford to buy. This was not to say that following the rules in a manufacturing process was expensive. The point was that the operators didn't see many of these rules as essential.

According to Charles, compliance with all rules—without any attempt to classify them as essential and inessential—was the key feature of Japanese manufacturing. This was behind the high yield and reliability of their microchips, as well as behind the high reliability of their cars and other products.

This may not seem logical when we think that mechanical engineering utilizes exact and well-established science. For example, the brakes constitute an important system of a car, so all the steps needed to make and assemble brakes should be very well understood. Not only mechanical engineers but also experienced technicians should know what is essential and what is not in a brakes system. Yet, it turns out the reality is different. When a company changes a car model—and with that it changes the recipe for making the brakes—errors do happen occasionally, and the companies recall their vehicles to rectify the problem. The mechanical theory needed to make car brakes is well established, but the theoretical knowledge is idealized to some extent. That's why any change from the old recipe is effectively a new trial that may end up as an error to be fixed when it's discovered at a later stage. The story with safety air bags is similar.

In general, any change in an established recipe is a new trial and a reliability risk. To ensure a high quality and a high reliability of a product, you should apply a verified recipe without any modifications. The logic that you can modify inessential steps in a recipe without a risk does not work. Ticking the key boxes is not sufficient. Seemingly irrelevant departures from a recipe frequently lead to poor-quality products and services. Smart thinking is not desirable when implementing a verified recipe. The best products and services follow strict recipes to ensure compliance with established and, frequently, legally defined standards.

Don't disregard inessential customer needs.

Similar to the fraught knowledge of essential and inessential recipe items, we have examples of failures due to the concept of essential customer needs. To avoid waste of valuable resources, communist governments of the Eastern Bloc of countries implemented a system of planned economies. Based on data about peoples' needs for food, clothing, and other essential items, the central governments of these countries established and followed strict plans for production, distribution, and pricing of all essential goods. Similar to the lean system of production and consumption, the idea was to avoid both oversupply and undersupply by providing exact quantities of goods at exactly the right time. Different from the lean system, the production was not according to customer demand but according to science-based models of peoples' needs.

What really happened were chronic shortages and surpluses. Long lines of people were a common sight. People lined up day after day for popular goods, without even knowing when the goods would eventually arrive. The things customers wanted to buy were different from the science of what they needed.

Another example is books, in the context of education being an essential need of every person. Qualified teachers select textbooks according to the needs of their students, but these essential reading materials don't dominate the number of published and sold books.

Richard Dawkins, an evolutionary biologist and science popularizer, explains in his 1976 book, *The Selfish Gene,*[36] why neither need nor purpose determine what dominates in nature. A simple example is how the notorious viruses impact our world through flu seasons, epidemics, and pandemics. This happens even though viruses are not proper living organisms, let alone able to infect us on purpose. What enables them to dominate us occasionally is the ability of their genes to self-replicate and to flood our human population with a colossal number of copies.

The idea that effective replication, rather than need or purpose, is crucial for numerical dominance extends beyond biology.

In analogy with the term *gene* for a unit of biological information, Dawkins coined the term *meme* for a unit of information that moves from one mind to another. His examples of memes stretch from the apparently purposeless wearing of a baseball cap backwards to the propagation of religious ideas. In general, a meme is any idea that passes from a person to person so easily that it appears as a self-replicating unit. Proverbs, witty quotes, and jokes are examples of memes that existed before the publication of *The Selfish Gene* in 1976, when Dawkins suggested the use of the term meme. With today's electronic communication, we have emoji memes and memes combining an image with a witty text.

In analogy with the numerical dominance of self-replicated genes, an idea becomes a meme if it's easy to pass it on. However, as distinct from genes, both need and purpose play a role in the case of memes. The natural selection in the process of gene replication is different from the cognitive selection in the case of memes. The genes of a biological virus spread simply because their purposeless self-replication trials are successful; in other words, they pile up in huge numbers simply because they can. In the case of memes as "cognitive viruses," the easiness of propagation is a helpful but not a sufficient criterion. Humans are able to pass many simple ideas to other people, but they select not to do it. A person usually decides to pass an idea to another person because of a perceived value of the idea. The value does not need to be as high as solving a pressing problem—it can be as simple as spreading a bit of fun—but the value has to be sufficient to justify the required effort.

Minimize versatility of the units you wish to replicate.

Having recognized that need and purpose play a role for propagation of human ideas, let's go back to take a look at the spontaneous mechanism of self-replication in biological cells. We can learn something from the simple trick of nature that creates copies of an immense number of symbols.

The immense number of symbols is about three billion, lined up in sequences as a set of 46 DNA molecules that make the unique genome of each person. About 2 percent of these symbols make our genes. If these three billion symbols were the alphanumeric characters in books, we would have about 4,000 books. It is estimated that a human body may have as many as a hundred trillion cells, and almost each of them has the complete genome with three billion symbols. In the analogy with the information contained in 4,000 books, this corresponds to a hundred trillion copies of each of these books.

Starting from a single cell, self-replications of all 46 DNA molecules in the genome and concurrent cell divisions create all these copies. Information coded by the DNA symbols provides instructions for the synthesis of proteins and other molecules during cell divisions. However, the self-replication mechanism of DNA molecules themselves is at the level of individual symbols. The key here is that a DNA molecule consists of two strands and the symbols from each strand connect each other by two distinct types of pairing bonds. The symbols are *A*, *C*, *G*, and *T*, from the first letters of the names for four respective molecules. The two types of pairing links are the double bond between *A* and *T* and the triple bond between *C* and *G*.

The bonds between the two strands are the weakest inter-atomic bonds in the DNA molecule and they occasionally break. If this happens in a soup of roaming *A*, *C*, *G*, and *T* units, a wandering *A* may hit a *G* in an apparent trial to form a group. However, this will not be a stable group and will quickly fall apart. In terms of the Anna Karenina principle, this is not a happy family. Happy families are the double bonds between *A* and *T* and the triple bonds between *C* and *G*. The random trials of short-lived pairs don't matter. What matters are the random encounters that form the stable double-bonded $A{=}T$ and triple-bonded $C{\equiv}G$ pairs. This is the self-replication trick that converts random trials into proper copies of the splitting DNA molecule. Exact sciences represent replications due to this kind of natural selection as "laws" of nature. In this example, a law of chemistry re-creates the DNA strands.

What we are learning here is that versatility is not a good attribute for replication. If the unit *A* could adapt to form bonds with *G* and *C*, not just with *T*, the described self-replication mechanism wouldn't work. In contrast, the inflexible matching of pairs turns the uncertainty of randomly moving units into the predictable self-replication. This is what creates order from chaos.

We can generalize this fundamental effect to say that adaptable recipes are not good for replication of products and adaptable messages don't travel too far. For reliable replication of products, we need frozen and clearly specified recipes. Likewise, if we wish to spread a message by the word of mouth, we have to make it unambiguous. If people have to interpret the message, they are not likely to put the effort and, even if they do, their interpretation is likely to be different from the intended effect.

Don't create unhappy families by ignoring the arrow of evolution.

It's possible that billions of years ago, before the first cell evolved, stand-alone $A=T$ and $C\equiv G$ pairs were floating in what is called primordial soup of organic molecules. However, the environment has changed and stand-alone pairs no longer exist. Yet, the numbers of $A=T$ and $C\equiv G$ pairs are larger than ever before, but as elements of the DNA molecules in most cells of all humans, animals, and plants.

This has happened only because the genes grouped spontaneously with other molecules to form cells; then varied cells grouped to form different organs, which make plants and animals. When the primordial soup disappeared, genes and DNA molecules can no longer replicate on their own without the needed molecules and energy. From the perspective of genes and DNA molecules, the complex functions of plants and animals supply food with the needed building blocks and energy so that they can replicate themselves. In return, the information coded by the DNA symbols guides the needed processes. This kind of teamwork enables our bodies to function, but the chain of growing complexity doesn't stop at individual bodies. No single human can survive without the knowledge that our complex society provides.

Each one of us is more than the sum of molecules, genes, and organs—so much so that we can find a spiritual purpose for our existence. However, the molecules and genes did not put us together because of that purpose. What happened was spontaneous assembly of random structures, including complex units consisting of simpler units. Most of these molecular structures died off. When the primordial soup vanished, genes and DNA molecules could no longer survive on their own. Genes that exist today are those that grouped into cells and complex organisms, which enabled them to adapt and self-replicate through changing environment.

According to Richard Dawkins's metaphor in *The Selfish Gene*, we exist because the genes needed us to survive and to continue their replication. To describe this effect in a straightforward and more general way, we can say that the arrow of evolution is from the simplest molecules toward the complex organisms and, finally, groups of organisms. Generalizing the metaphor of selfish units, we can say that we as individuals create teams for the sake of our own survival and prosperity.

Teams and large organizations function as more than the sum of individuals. These groups regard their holistic functions as the purpose of their existence. However, no group's purpose can turn around the arrow of evolution and erase the deep-rooted evolutionary selfishness of individuals. People create unhappy families when they fail to recognize this reality.

4

Differences are the Key When the Conditions Change

Happy families are alike, but they change over time. Evolution never stops and the environment changes, so the happy families today are not the same as in the past. To emphasize this point in the context of competition between companies, Peter Thiel, an entrepreneur and the author of *Zero to One*, contrasted Tolstoy's sentence about similarities between happy families. He stated that "all happy companies are different" and all unhappy companies are alike in that they failed to escape competition.[37]

Thiel's focus on the differences between companies doesn't mean that any random difference can create a happy company. In short, doing everything right, according to existing knowledge, eventually leads to unhappy companies. The point is about the need to evolve and innovate.

Accept that knowledge cannot eliminate the need for uncertain trials.

Before Henry Ford popularized the business model of mass production, companies built their cars in response to specific orders by individual customers. There was no fixed recipe; instead, different people applied their knowledge and skills as they worked with sophisticated equipment to create custom-designed cars. Making cars by this type of craft was typical in American industry at the time, but Ford saw a problem: The cars were far too expensive and inaccessible to middle-class Americans. He decided to slash the cost per manufactured car by implementing the mass-production method in his company. In his own words, the "way to make automobiles is to make one automobile like another automobile, to make them all alike," just as "one match is like another match when it comes from the match factory."[38]

However, Ford's successful introduction of mass production had to evolve through trials of many car prototypes that did not make it to the mass-production phase. Ford's selection of features for his Ford Model A, which was made in 1903 and 1904, brought about a scant success. The sales were just sufficient to enable the company to continue developing new models. Mechanical problems plagued Model A, and it took several trials with subsequent models to find adequate solutions for these problems. In addition to that, Ford didn't know the exact features and cost that the potential customers would accept. He tried one prototype after another, most of them not reaching the production line. The next model that was a moderate success was Model N, followed by Models R and S. The big success was Model T, which Ford released in 1908 and kept in production until 1927. This was the first mass-produced and affordable car that middle-class Americans accepted.

One of the reasons Ford had to try so many models before the big success was the lack of technical knowledge and the need to try solutions for various mechanical problems. But, the lack of sufficient *technical* knowledge wasn't the only reason for risky trials. In addition to the technical trials, Ford was testing customers' acceptance of different features at different price levels, which poses the following question: Couldn't he ask the potential customers about the price they would accept and the features they would like to have?

This seems like a good question because innovation by risky trials is expensive. However, the premise of the question is false because customers may not be able to tell whether they would like specific features of a product that does not exist. Customers can say what they need, but this information is in the context of existing products and it will change as new products appear. That is why Ford had to try specific car models and then to evolve the next model based on customers' acceptance and feedback.

Understand why successful recipes are not eternal.

Following the great acceptance of Model T, Ford decided to end the evolution of new models and to focus on improving the production efficiency to reduce cost and to increase the sales. He decided to implement the model of mass production with Model T. Once the customers accepted the features of the car, Ford was able to freeze the production recipe and to standardize the needed knowledge and skills. Over time, this reduced the manpower needed for manufacturing while increasing the production rate, which dropped the price per car from more than 800 dollars to less than 300 dollars. The successful run with this model lasted 19 years, resulting in more than 15 million sold cars.

Ford took this extraordinary success as an *experimental proof* that the design was "perfect," offering everything that a customer would ever need from a car. Based on this experimental evidence, he ignored the attempts by competitors to offer new features in terms of comfort and styling. He resisted his son's pleas to introduce innovative styling and to upgrade the performance of Model T.

Ford ignored the only certainty about the future, which is the fact that the things will change.

The competition to Model T changed consumer tastes. Flashy paint and special trims emerged as selling features. People started joking that you could go anywhere in a Model T, except in society. Americans were turning to products with individuality and style as a way of escaping the dullness of their factory lives.[39] Ford Motor Company was losing the share of US car market, from two thirds in 1924 to one third by late 1926. On May 26, 1927, manufacturing of Model T ended. Ford closed all his factories around to world for six months to change the Model-T tools and to prepare the design of a new car.

People do want a high degree of certainty. In the example of cars, this means they want a reliable operation. However, it's an overgeneralization to think that people's need for certainty means they don't need surprises. Humans have evolved with an innate desire for changes. We play games and watch movies to satisfy our innate need for surprises. We take a risk to make a change. It's risky to buy a product with different features from a proven model. However, people will take the risk if it provides a balanced difference that satisfies their need for surprising changes. Obviously, customers cannot specify the surprise they want, but that doesn't mean customers only want what they can tell you. It certainly doesn't mean they want an identical product forever.

Understand that perfection is a trap in the face of change.

The change in customer taste that ended the reign of Ford's Model T was gradual, which made it predictable in the short term. This enabled General Motors—a Ford competitor—to act preemptively and to offer new features that people desired.

In general, it's a standard management practice to rely on the ability to detect and model slowly changing environments, and then to prepare plans for anticipated new conditions. Of course, math has to be used to make quantified predictions. Everyone can do simple extrapolations of recent trends, but they are only good for short-term predictions. In contrast to this primitive approach, economist Richard M. Goodwin's model of business cycles illustrates the preferred use of calculus.[40] According to this model, a high level of employment drives up the wages, which shrinks the profits and consequently reduces the employment. As the reduced employment drops down the wages, profits increase and the increasing employment drives up the wages again in a new cycle of growth and decline.

Goodwin's mathematical model consists of two simple calculus equations. Biologists use the same equations to model predator–prey relationships. An example is a population of identical foxes as predators and a population of identical rabbits as prey. The foxes eat only rabbits, so an increase in the number of foxes causes a decrease in the number of rabbits, which then causes a decline in the number of foxes; once the number of rabbits recovers, the number of foxes increases again and a new cycle of decline and growth begins.

As distinct from straightforward extrapolations, these examples illustrate that calculus models can account for cycles and turnarounds. The cycles in these examples are idealized, because the simple set of equations assumes fixed overall conditions. However, calculus-based models can be made more complex to involve time-variable conditions and additional parameters. Humans have developed and successfully used very complex systems of this type of equations in areas spanning from engineering design to climate-change predictions.

For example, the simple fox-and-rabbit model can be upgraded to predict the impact of added specimens of smarter foxes. The ability of these foxes to catch and eat rabbits at a higher rate will increase their population, but it will progressively reduce the number of rabbits. Then, it may happen that the foxes eat the last remaining rabbit, which will also exterminate the whole fox population. This prediction illustrates how a stronger competitor can tip the balance off to cause unsustainable changes.

We have a different scenario if a random gene mutation creates a new breed of foxes, which eat rats in addition to rabbits. The population of foxes with the new gene will grow at a higher rate compared to the foxes with the original gene. Because the new foxes eat rabbits, not just rats, they will compete with the old foxes whose population will decrease.

The new species of fox is a formidable competitor, but it brings diversity and it doesn't compete on strength alone. To illustrate what difference its diversity can make, let's introduce a catastrophic random event in the environment—for example, a lightning event that sets off fire and burns all the grass. Although both rabbits and rats survive in their burrows, the rabbit population dies off without the grass, whereas many rats are able to find food and survive. No mathematical modeling could predict such a black-swan event. However, we don't need modeling to see that, with no rabbits, total extinction of the unaltered fox species is the result of the random lightning event. Under the scenario of *perfect* replication of the original fox genes, which means without the random mutation that created the new diversified fox, the complete pool of fox genes would disappear. It is the replication errors in a single gene— the mutation that created the rat-eating foxes—what enabled all the other genes in the pool to survive.

This example takes us to a fundamental point: Striving for perfection is a tragic survival strategy, because it ignores unpredictable changes. Perfection is incompatible with novelty—necessary for any chance of adaptation to changed conditions. It is neither the most perfect nor the strongest who will survive, but rather those who can best manage change.

The method of random adaptability to randomly changing conditions is fundamental. It's impossible to adapt to unpredictable changes without trying something different. Trying new things creates diversity, which may not serve any concurrent need. However, diversity creates options before it becomes too late to try new things. A real-life example for this point is Intel's development of the first microprocessors when the market didn't need them, which was later their only survival option in the face of deadly competition from Japanese companies.

Keep in mind that it may be easier to create than to predict change.

Intel was founded in 1968 as a start-up company with the idea of utilizing the newly evolving semiconductor technology. The core technical idea was a placement of computer memories on a single silicon chip. They had the first commercial success in 1970, when a large computer company decided to replace the old devices with their new product. Memory chips quickly became the standard technology worldwide, because they were much cheaper and used less power than the old technology. Intel continued to develop and introduce better memory products, and for more than a decade, Intel meant memories and semiconductor memories meant Intel.

Growing from a start-up company to a large manufacturer, Intel built many factories and employed people to run these production facilities. The task of engineers and technicians in these factories was to implement and control complex processing, with the ultimate aim of delivering products with as tight specs as possible.

Speaking in general, people who would take risks with new ideas are not suitable for these production tasks. The suitable people feel happy when everything runs in the same way as it has been in the past. These are do-it-by-the-book characters who detest surprises at work. They dislike departures from their valuable knowledge. In a sentence, the central value for them is the degree of similarity between the outcomes and the established knowledge of what the outcomes should be.

In contrast, people who develop new things value outcomes that are different from existing knowledge. In Intel's example, a big difference between the idea for memory chips and the existing memory technology was the tempting big value for the company pioneers. For them, this was a difference that could make a big impact on the market. It required an engagement with uncertainty, but its value was worth the risk they were taking.

The breed of people who pursue new ideas have a thick skin for what others see as repeated failures. Unworkable new ideas keep popping up in their minds and they have to screen them out, but even the ideas they share with colleagues don't necessarily work as presented. This is unavoidable because ideas, like any other new trials, originate from random events. The unpredictability of a random trial guarantees its novelty, but successful new trials are rare even though they do happen. Describing how a random mutation was the only way foxes could survive the catastrophic black-swan event, we focused on a lucky mutation. What we need to keep in mind is that such a mutation would emerge from an immense number of trials, just as a happy lottery winner emerges from the forgotten misery of many losers.

There are many more ways to make an unfavorable random change, and the only good thing about these trials is that they don't have a lasting impact. The random trails that make a desirable difference are extremely rare.

With this in mind, it would seem logical for the management of a successful company not to waste resources on random trials. However, that wasn't the case at Intel. Aside from the production people, they kept engineers in their research and development department. It did make sense to keep evolving new memory products, which enabled a healthy growth of sales. However, they were also spending money on a group of people to play with the idea of microprocessors.

Similar to memories, a microprocessor on a single chip could make a big difference in terms of significantly reduced cost and size of computers. Different from memory chips, the market for microprocessors seemed to be far too small to justify the costly and long-term investment in their development. This was around the 1970s, and no one could foresee the use of microprocessors in today's smart phones and personal computers. In fact, the engineers and all other experts at the time couldn't even see that personal computers would be used as smart typewriters. The first microprocessors that Intel's engineers developed in the early 1970s were too primitive for such a task. A good illustration of the knowledge and thinking at the time is the view of Ken Olsen—a co-founder of Digital Equipment Corporation and the person who took the industry from large mainframe computers to networks of smaller and cheaper minicomputers. He thought that "the personal computer will fall flat on its face in business," and voiced the following opinion in 1977: "There is no reason for any individual to have a computer in his home."[41]

The market for microprocessors wasn't there, and the memory business was growing safely for Intel. To not put all their eggs in one basket, they entered the growing digital watch market in 1972. It was a failure and they sold this business with a loss in 1978. Yet, they continued to invest in the development of microprocessors, in spite of the lack of a justifiable market on the horizon.

Intel's business was run by its two co-founders and a co-developer of the memory technology: Gordon Moore, a chemist, Robert Noyce, a physicist and a co-inventor of the integrated circuit, and Andrew Grove, a chemical engineer. With their technical background and innovation mindset, they valued the difference that microprocessors could make for small and affordable, yet functionally powerful computers. The lack of identifiable market and the view that the idea for a personal computer wouldn't fly did not deter them from spending some of their cash for a technical progress with their microprocessors. A dry investor would see this as a stupid market risk for the love of the technology. However, this is not quite true if we keep in mind that they didn't borrow the money to play the microprocessor game. We all spend some of the money we earn for things we like. In their case, they were spending their own money not only on something they valued but also on something that had the potential to create a huge business in the future.

Intel's management had no reason to suspect any serious problems with their memory business, apart from the generic idea not to put all eggs in one basket. Competitors were emerging, but Intel was still by far the dominant player on the market. The company image was unshakable, the production culture was strong and improving, and better memory products were rolling off the development chain. No one could predict that Japanese producers could make chips with 100 percent yield, which meant both cheaper and higher-quality products. As Grove tells us in his book *Only the Paranoid Survive*,[42] Intel fought hard. They improved the quality and brought costs down but the Japanese producers fought back. Intel tried to focus on a niche segment of the memory market, tried to invent special-purpose memories, introduced more advanced technologies, but nothing worked. The Japanese weapon of high-quality product priced astonishingly low was unbeatable.

While this fight was going on, Intel continued to play the microprocessor game. It was a diverse egg as a different product but, without a profitable market, there was no basket to put it in. However, it started to look like a golden egg in 1981 when International Business Machines (IBM) chose Intel's latest microprocessor for IBM's first mass-produced personal computer. This was more than ten years of microprocessor development, and exactly ten years after their first attempt to grow this market with their first commercial product.

This success was a glimmer of hope, but the company was against the wall with their losses in the dominant memory business. It was hard for Gordon Moore and Andrew Grove as the top executives to cut the losses and halt memory production. Emotionally, it was going to be like losing company's identity. Operationally, memory processing was in the blood of most production staff. As Grove writes, rational discussion about getting out of memories was practically impossible. Managers at all levels believed the memory technology was their "technology driver," and they couldn't see how Intel could function without its backbone. However, the cruel reality was that the memory road was well and truly blocked by Japanese competitors. The only hope was the diversity of microprocessors. Moore and Grove decided to abandon the memory business and to shift completely to microprocessors as the new corporate strategy.

Intel created the future in early 1970's with their memory products. They reincarnated the company in 1985 by creating their future again as the microprocessor company. They could do it because the management kept investing in their innovators—the breed of people who cherish differences from existing knowledge.

Speaking in general, betting on differences is fairly easy. Even lottery players do it when they stay away from past winning combinations. However, innovators play much smarter games. They analyze differences and generalize simi-larities to shape realistic new ideas. This means they think.

Let's take a look at some examples to unveil the key thinking trick.

PART B

The Intelligence Level

5

Think by Analyzing Differences before Generalizing Similarities

Politicians, business leaders, consultants, and motivational speakers like to quote the following sentence from a speech that John F. Kennedy's gave in 1959: "When written in Chinese, the word 'crisis' is composed of two characters—one represents danger and one represents opportunity."[43]

The idea that a crisis can create opportunities is a great meme for some people. Yet, others mock it as either political spin or wishful thinking. These opposing views reflect two distinct cognitive attributes, which William James—the first educator to offer a psychology course in the United States—described as (1) "reasoning" and (2) "associative wisdom":

Reasoning helps us out of unprecedented situations—situations for which all our common associative wisdom, all the "education" which we share in common with the beasts, leaves us without resource.[44]

A simple example can illustrate these two attributes. A chef in a restaurant receives a meal order from a couple of regular customers. The order is for their standard parmesan-crusted salmon with asparagus, but it sends danger signals through the chef's brain. He used all asparagus the day before and forgot about it. In the absence of any reasoning, his culinary education cannot help him. The obvious option is to apologize and to ask the customers to order something else. After some thinking, however, the chef decides to offer a new version of the dish, which would be parmesan-crusted salmon with mushrooms and leeks.

In principle, no two cuts of salmon are the same and no two plates of a salmon dish can be identical, but we ignore these differences as irrelevant. We *generalize similarities* to say that the salmon cuts are the same. However, we wouldn't say that salmon with mushrooms is the same dish as salmon with asparagus. This difference matters.

With this difference, the chef is taking a risk. The proposed version of the dish is not on the menu and he hasn't cooked it for a while. Even if he manages to do it well, the customers may not like it. But it also opens the opportunity to delight the customers with the suggested change. If this happens, it would be an example of what *Harry Potter* author J.K. Rowling has said: Every success begins with a failure.

This chapter is about thinking that can help us out of unprecedented situations, can help us solve problems, adapt to change, innovate, and see opportunities in a crisis. This kind of thinking makes the difference between intelligence and dumb reliance on existing knowledge to act in an unknown situation.

To trigger thinking, spot and analyze differences.

Thinking is disheartening when we don't know where to start this process. A dumb use of what we know rather well is the easy way out. The famous Monty Hall problem is an excellent example to illustrate this point.

Inspired by the television show *Let's Make a Deal*, hosted by Monty Hall, a professor from the University of California, Berkley, formulated this problem in a Letter to the Editor of the *American Statistician* in 1975.[45] The solution of the problem sparked a passionate debate fifteen years later when a reader rephrased the original problem to ask the following succinct question:

> Dear Marilyn:
>
> Suppose you're on a game show, and you're given the choice of three doors. Behind one door is a car, behind the others, goats. You pick a door, say number 1, and the host, who knows what's behind the doors, opens another door, say number 3, which has a goat. He says to you, "Do you want to pick door number 2?" Is it to your advantage to switch your choice of doors.[46]

Consistent with the solution in the original letter, Marilyn answered that the chance of winning is two in three by switching to door number 2, which is higher than the chance of one in three for door number 1. This answer flies in the face of the wisdom associating doors 1 and 2 with the equal head and tail choices in the analogous coin-flipping scenario. To use James's terminology, this is an example where the associative wisdom is faster but inferior to reasoning.

After posting her answer, and even after offering a follow-up explanation, Marilyn received thousands of patronizing letters from prominent experts. Here is one from a Georgetown University professor, Dr. E. Ray Bobo:

You are utterly incorrect about the game show question, and I hope this controversy will call some public attention to the serious national crisis in mathematical education. How many irate mathematicians are needed to get you to change your mind?[47]

The chance that Marilyn made the right choice by picking door 1 is one in three and, in that case, she would lose by her decision to switch. On the other hand, the chance that the car is not behind door 1 is two in three, which becomes the chance to win the car by switching from the initial choice of door 1. Ignoring the fact that Monty Hall eliminated the third choice by opening door 3, the choice between doors 1 and 2 appears analogous to the equal coin-flipping probabilities. However, the ignored fact makes a difference because Monty would have opened door 2 if the car were behind door 3, in which case the decision to switch to the then available door 3 would be also a win.

This thinking is from the point of view of a contestant who has one opportunity to play the game, without the possibility to run repeated experiments and to calculate probabilities from their outcomes. However, it's easy to perform repeated analogous experiments, and that is what Marilyn asked math classes across the country to do. Following her call, many excited teachers wrote about their experience, all confirming that switching resulted in wins in about 67 percent of trials.

Presented with two options, door 1 or door 2, most people tend to ignore the detail that Monty opened door 3. It would be the first step of James's reasoning to analyze what difference the opening of door 3 makes, but that would require time, effort, and some healthy doubt in math expertise. It would be the first step of *slow thinking* in the terminology of Daniel Kahneman, a psychologist who won the 2002 Nobel Prize in Economic Sciences, and the author of *Thinking, Fast and Slow.*[48]

This process would have to evolve slowly through back-and-forth neuron firing in the brain's grey matter. Richard Thaler and Cass Sunstein, the authors of *Nudge*,[49] assign this process to what they call "reflective system" of our brain.

In contrast to thinking about the difference that opening of door 3 could make, the strength of the wisdom associating doors 1 and 2 with the familiar head and tail choices leads to what Kahneman calls "fast thinking." In this case, our "automatic system"—in Thaler and Sunstein's terminology—executes the fast, effortless, and wrong decision that the probabilities are equal.

The strength of knowledge, residing in our automatic system, makes it easy to ignore relevant differences and, consequently, makes it harder to both think and learn. It can make learning so unlikely that even pigeons learn faster when presented with Monty-Hall type of choices; and they do it not because they are smarter than humans but because their small brains are less polluted with strong knowledge.

In 2010, psychologists Walter T. Herbranson and Julia Schroeder published a paper entitled "Are Birds Smarter than Mathematicians?"[50], which investigated whether pigeons, like most humans, would fail to maximize their expected winnings in a version of Monty-Hall choices. They used three pecking keys and a feeder through which birds could gain access to mixed grain. At the beginning of a trial, a computer randomly linked one of the three keys to the feeder and illuminated all three keys with white light. After the bird pecked any one of the lit keys, the computer followed Monty-Hall's scheme to deactivate and darken one of the keys, in analogy with the door opening in the game. The key that the bird pecked and the additional active key were then illuminated with green light. If a bird then pecked the key that the computer selected initially as the prize key, it was given a short access to the mixed grain before starting a new trial.

For a comparison, Herbranson and Schroeder performed analogous experiments with undergraduates at Whitman College, where the two were on the faculty. The students were not informed about the Monty Hall problem.

The results are unambiguous. At the beginning, the pigeons switched from the initially pecked key about a third of the time. As the trials proceeded, the pigeons learned that switching from the original choice resulted in a better chance to access the grain.

Not knowing anything about the Monty Hall problem, the students' initial rate of switching was close to the coin-flipping probability of 50 percent. The knowledge that the choice between two illuminated keys is analogous to coin flipping seemed to inhibit students' learning. Unlike the pigeons, whose switching rate was nearly 100 percent, the students only improved slightly, reaching just 66 percent.

Like most other people, the students kept ignoring the relevant difference between coin-flipping probabilities and Monty-Hall problem. Yet some differences matter and the first step in a thinking process is to identify them. After that, the process is to decide how to deal with them.

The decision what to do with a relevant difference—once it's identified—is often obvious. The following hypothetical example illustrates again that the most important thinking trick is not to ignore a relevant difference in the first place. In the example, we have a restaurant manager who wants to quantify the demand for three different types of salad dressings offered by the restaurant. Recorded choices of recent customers show that a hundred people selected option A, seventy picked option B, and thirty went for option C. A side note stated that two customers asked for a reduced-salt dressing, even though this possibility was not on the list. These two unexpected responses correspond to one percent of the two hundred recorded selections. However, this mathematically correct calculation does not mean that only one percent of customers would order a reduced-salt dressing if offered in the future. A proper analysis of the difference that reduced-salt options could make is likely to show that offering these options would be attractive to a significant number of customers. The manager would be ignoring a signal for business opportunity by interpreting the two unexpected responses as only one percent of customers' choices.

Do not ignore differences that can make a big difference.

Describing his discovery of penicillin, Alexander Fleming provides a historic example of missed opportunities due to the common failure to analyze unexpected outcomes. According to Fleming, he was not the first lucky person to stumble upon the effect of destructed bacterial colonies by *Penicillium* mold. He makes the following statement in a paper recounting his discovery: "It is certain that every bacteriologist has not once but many times had culture plates contaminated with moulds."[51] According to Fleming, this made it probable that some bacteriologists had noticed suppressed bacterial growth around contaminating mold well before he observed this phenomenon on September 28, 1928. However, in the absence of any special interest in naturally occurring antibacterial substances, these bacteriologists did not analyze the unexpected observations; instead, they simply discarded the contaminated cultures as failed experiments. Fleming was fortunate because he was always on the lookout for new bacterial inhibitors, following his previous work on natural antibacterial substances. Consequently, he was sufficiently interested to analyze the unexpected absence of bacterial colonies when one of his culture plates accidentally grew mold while Fleming was on a summer vacation.

Acknowledging that Fleming's discovery of penicillin changed the course of medicine, medical experts still describe it as a series of chance events of almost unbelievable improbability.[52] Far from denying the role of chance in new discoveries, we should recognize that the element of chance is necessary—nothing new can happen by replication of past events and by mere application of existing knowledge. However, the improbability of specific chance events is not the key obstacle. Even if we use the analogy with lottery when thinking about Fleming's chance to find a rare strain of bacteria-suppressing mold, we should not ignore that—in this analogy—Fleming was not the only lottery player. Contaminated culture plates were lottery tickets for every bacteriologist and some of them included the winning combination of depleted staphylococcal colonies around *Penicillium* mold. However, these bacteriologists were like illiterate lottery players who could not read their lucky combination, which was the actual discovery obstacle.

None of us is short of "lottery tickets" and their sheer abundance is a problem because we cannot analyze them all. The abundance of daily random events begins when we wake up and become aware of unbelievable random combinations and links in our dreams. However, analyzing the new elements in our dreams is rarely useful for the future reality. Soon after we wake up, perhaps while showering, random ideas pop up in our mind. We remember the most promising idea but, being new, it begins to feel like a square peg in a round hole when confronted with everyday reality. We forget the idea, not allowing randomness to infect our mind.

Strict quality-control procedures strongly discourage any randomness in the work activities of many people. Most people work consciously and persistently to create well-controlled environment, free from undesired uncertainty. However, if Fleming controlled the processes in his lab so tightly to prevent mold contamination of his culture plates, he would not have discovered penicillin.

Some random events turn into seeds of discovery and

innovation, and we shouldn't inhibit them by excessive control. On the other hand, most random events will not result in useful seeds and many can be quite harmful if not prevented. As we already acknowledged, bad luck is far more frequent than good luck. Therefore, business-minded people should be aware that a discovery of a lucky seed is a rare opportunity to grow it into a rewarding innovation. Yet so many people lack this awareness and abandon their luck too early. The story of penicillin is a good example. Fleming published his findings in 1929 and gave the name "penicillin" to the active agent in the mold,[53] but he did not isolate penicillin for clinical use. He sent his *Penicillium* mold to anyone who requested it so that others could try, but nothing happened for the next ten years.

It is insightful to think why Fleming and so many others ended up ignoring the difference that penicillin could make with its potential to prevent death from common bacterial infections. Lack of funding and other resources in London's St Mary's Hospital where Fleming worked is a possible reason, but lack of money cannot be the reason for all potential investors and for rich people who were donating money to various charities. It seems the problem was the *lack of certainty* that money could turn the published discovery into a clinical antibiotic. Uncertain about a successful development of this drug, and uncertain whether they would ever need it, rich people could not see their potential donations as an insurance against a deadly infection in the future. Thinking that the transition from Fleming's mold to a marketable antibiotic was highly uncertain, investors could not see it as a great business opportunity. With poorly analyzed and overrated uncertainty, nobody saw an opportunity in Fleming's discovery for almost a decade.

The situation with the forgotten penicillin began to change in 1938 when Ernst Chain, working under supervision of Howard Florey at Oxford University, found Fleming's

1929 publication. As a professor of pathology, Florey was curious about long-known observations that bacteria and fungi were capable of killing each other. He was also a master of extracting research funding from both government and industry bodies. Fleming's strain of *Penicillium* mold had been saved at Oxford and Florey assembled a team to begin work on the link between fungi and death of bacteria. In addition to Chain, who successfully purified penicillin from a mold extract, the team included Norman Heatley who worked on growing large amounts of Fleming's strain of *Penicillium* mold. In 1940, Florey carried out successful experiments with mice and in February 1941 tried to cure a 43-year old patient from a life-threatening infection. Injected penicillin led to a remarkable recovery within days but supplies of the drug ran out and the patient died a few days later.

Florey was facing the problem that thousands of liters of mold fluid were needed to extract enough pure penicillin to treat a single person. The war-absorbed chemical industry in Britain couldn't help, so Florey turned to the Rockefeller Foundation and, receiving their support, he travelled with Heatley to the United States in the summer of 1941. The aim was to instigate the interest of the American pharmaceutical industry. While Florey was visiting companies such as Merck and Pfizer, Heatley worked with the foremost authorities on the *Penicillium* mold and fermentation processing at Northern Regional Research Laboratory (NRRL) in Peoria, Illinois. Trying various new techniques, the initial work at NRRL significantly increased the yield of penicillin from Fleming's strain of *Penicillium* mold.

Nonetheless, this was not sufficient and soon a global search was underway for better penicillin producing strains. Samples arrived at NRRL from around the world, but it was a local laboratory assistant who brought the most productive strain from a Peoria fruit market in the form of a moldy cantaloupe. Subsequent use of X-rays at the Carnegie Institution resulted in even more productive mutant of the cantaloupe strain, and still better mutation was obtained by exposure to ultraviolet radiation at the University of Wisconsin.

In the meantime, Florey was disappointed by the initial results of his company visits. Then he decided to visit his friend Alfred Newton Richards, who was chairing a national committee on medical research relating to national defense. Richards told the drug companies who expressed some interest during Florey's visits (Merck, Squibb, Lilly, and Pfizer) "that they would be serving the national interest if they undertook penicillin production and that there might be support from the federal government."[54] These companies remained skeptical after a meeting in Washington, D.C., in October of 1941, but their thinking changed at a conference organized by Richards's committee in New York in December of 1941—ten days after the attack on Pearl Harbor and US entry into World War II.

By March 1942, Merck supplied enough penicillin to treat the first patient successfully. In June 1942, there was enough penicillin to treat ten additional cases. Production of penicillin in the United States reached 21 billion units in 1943, jumped to 1,663 billion units in 1944, and to more than 6.8 trillion units in 1945.[55]

In 1945, Alexander Fleming, Howard Florey, and Ernst Chain received the Nobel Prize for the impact of their penicillin research and development.

It took diverse thinking by different people to turn penicillin from Fleming's curiosity into a life-saving drug. Chance events did play a role, but the common perception of their improbability illustrates a lack of proper uncertainty analysis.

The initial chance event was the accidental growth of *Penicillium* mold, which killed staphylococcal colonies in Fleming's culture plates while he was on a summer vacation.

However, as Fleming noted, it was probable that mold was also killing bacteria in the dishes of other bacteriologists. Therefore, the discovery obstacle was not a low probability of these unexpected events but the failure of bacteriologists to analyze them.

Another chance event was the transition from the original strain of mold to the high-yield mold, found on the cantaloupe that a lab assistant brought from a fruit market. However, this was after the progress on penicillin extraction from Fleming's strain stalled at inadequate yield levels, and the technical team decided to initiate a global search for better penicillin producing strains. Two important attributes of proper uncertainty analysis underlie this decision of the technical team:

1. their awareness that many trials would fail and
2. their awareness that at least one successful trial was likely and that it would make a big difference.

As it happened, the lab assistant brought the best-yielding cantaloupe mold coincidentally, but this was not the only possibility for a successful trial. Many other possibilities could have brought either the cantaloupe or another good-yield mold to the attention of the alert researchers.

The businesspeople assessed the uncertainty differently. Before the New York conference, which was held soon after the attack on Pearl Harbor, George W. Merck had been pessimistic about the possibility of producing adequate quantities of penicillin. The reason for this pessimism was unavailability of fermentation techniques for large volumes of low-yield mold. Merck and others did not see the lack of large-volume fermentation as an opportunity but as an intolerable risk. Florey and Richards had been using the national-defense argument, but it is possible that, without the unexpected Pearl Harbor attack, the progress reported at the New York conference would not have convinced them to begin work on penicillin production.

In hindsight, it is clear that the largest obstacle was due to very different assessments of the project uncertainty by the technical team and by company executives. This gap is frequently a critical obstacle.

An example when this gap did not exist was Edison's development of marketable incandescent lamp, and that's because Edison was both the technical and business decision maker. Otherwise, there are similarities between the uncertainty assessments during his global search for a long-lasting filament and during the global search for a better penicillin-producing mold.

We are trained to quantify uncertainty of future events by calculating probabilities from the outcomes of past experiments, but this can be misleading. After Edison's trials of ten filaments, all of which failed, the calculation of probability to fail was ten out of ten, or one hundred percent. This calculation remained the same after Edison tried a hundred and even after he tried a thousand filaments. However, the certainty of failure, implied by these calculations, was not Edison's assessment. He didn't ignore the rather large differences in lifetimes obtained by different filament materials. He correctly interpreted these results as a large uncertainty in lifetimes of as yet untried materials and—crucially—he saw this uncertainty as an opportunity to find a long-lasting filament.

Likewise, the research team at NRRL knew that the penicillin yield was very different for different molds, and they correctly interpreted this uncertain yield as an opportunity to find a suitable mold.

Differences and uncertainty could mean a great opportunity. This is the key insight from both the penicillin and lightbulb examples of turning uncertainty into business successes.

Distinguish generalizations with and without specific meaning.

Differences that we as humans cherish, and even exaggerate, relate to our own possessions. We easily distinguish the properties that we own from similar properties belonging to others. This also applies to the concept of intellectual property, which has to be different from the intellectual properties belonging to other people. When defining intellectual property in the form of patents, the patent attorneys attempt to fence as large ground as possible by formulating as general claims as possible. However, the key here is in the specific knowledge of what is possible.

Patents and patent claims can be quite technical, but we can illustrate the importance of *specific meaning* of a concept by the following simplified example. Consider that, some time ago, a company designed a hybrid electric vehicle to offer an affordable and practical solution for improved fuel efficiency. If successful on the market, other companies would be tempted to offer hybrid electric vehicles with different features: rear-wheel drive instead of front-wheel drive, diesel engine instead of gas engine, eight seats instead of five seats, and so on. A patent claiming the ownership of a specific feature that is common for all hybrid electric vehicles could protect the market for the company developing the new vehicle. Assume now that the following words are considered as the definition of the new specific feature: "a combination of a fuel-combustion engine and an electric motor." With this definition, differences in the type of fuel-combustion engine, in the number of seats, and so on, are irrelevant because all these different versions of vehicles would be classified as hybrid electric vehicles.

Performing the necessary search, the company's patent attorney is likely to discover that, in the early twentieth century, Porsche used electric motors in racing cars. The cars were driven by the electric motor alone; however, a fuel-combustion engine was used to run an electric generator to power the electric motor. Because the fuel-combustion engine is not mechanically driving the car, this is a different combination from the intended meaning of the new combination, which enables both the fuel-combustion engine and the electric motor to drive a vehicle. Nonetheless, the intended meaning is not demarcated by a proper difference from Porsche's combination. The phrase "a combination of a fuel-combustion engine and an electric motor" can be interpreted as Porsche's use of a fuel-combustion engine to power an electric motor.

The generic concept "a combination of" can mean different things to different people. Consequently, the attempt to fence unexplored ground by not specifying the combination would backfire.

Ignorance of specifics can be also a problem for generic managers. As an example, assume that the quality-control manager of a car manufacturer is informed about an unusual mechanical failure of a specific car. It may seem logical that the manager could ignore this information because his job is not to deal with specific incidents but to set up a general quality-control procedure. With this approach, however, the manager is unable to see that the cause of the *unusual* failure may be due to an omission in his general procedure. For example, the procedure may have omitted instructions to the production staff not to change the supplier of a specific part without a proper testing of the new part. Such an omission in the general procedure may remain undiscovered until the growing damage forces the quality-control manager to take the ultimate responsibility for the incurred loss.

It may seem impossible for a general manager to deal with specific failures, simply because of the sheer volume of cars and number of failures. If you are thinking that way, then you are at a general level where you are ignoring the difference between unusual failures and repeated failures. Yet, this difference is important because the manager doesn't need to think about the already known and classified mechanical failures. Mechanics in the service departments can apply existing knowledge to identify and fix known problems. Thinking is only required in the case of new failures, the ones eluding explanation by existing knowledge, and it is the small number of these specific failures that the manager shouldn't ignore.

To be able to think, a general manager must be able to analyze differences between new information and existing knowledge, which means the manager needs to possess that knowledge. Of course, no one can be an expert in all areas. So, what happens when a general manager does not possess the specific knowledge needed to deal with new information? In that case, the options available to the manager are to acquire the needed knowledge or to make random decisions.

Needed knowledge can be acquired in many ways, including by seeking an expert advice. Assume that the quality-control manager hires an adviser to analyze a specific and unusual mechanical failure. During this analysis, the adviser may come up with an idea for a new method to avoid this type of failures in the future. With this in mind, the manager states in their legal contract that any intellectual property developed by the adviser during the analysis will belong to the manager's company.

Irrespective of the specific clauses, such a contract cannot deliver automatic control to the company because the adviser physically owns his or her ideas; physically, these ideas are in the synapses of the adviser's brain. Furthermore, the ownership is exclusive because nobody else knows about the adviser's ideas. The adviser cannot utilize the new method without the company's cars, so it may seem that the manager has the practical control. However, the situation can change if the adviser is able to generalize the specific idea and to develop an adapted version of the method for a car model of a different manu-facturer. The adviser can then decide not to develop the new method for the manager who is paying for a mere analysis and to pursue a more favorable contract with a different car manufacturer.

You can generalize specific insight and benefit from the generalization, but you can easily lose when doing the oppo-site: relying on generalizations without specific meaning. In the previous example, the general but meaningless intellec-tual-property clause was not useful to the general manager.

To illustrate further this point about generalization of a specific insight, take the example of reported health bene-fits of omega-3 fatty acids, in particular two long-chain types common in fish oil. Numerous studies emerged reporting health benefits across a broad range of seemingly disconnected conditions: improved blood circulation, reduced blood pres-sure, reduced risk of heart attack and cardiac arrhythmias, reduced pain due to inflamed joints (rheumatoid arthri-tis), help with depression, reduced memory impairment (Alzheimer's disease), improvement in immune function, reduced risk of cancers and slowed cancer progression, and more. It is easy to generalize these reports in a statement that consuming the omega-3 fatty acids found in fish oil has broad health benefits. However, the absence of a specific underlying link between these diverse effects leaves this generalization open to a considerable doubt.

An oncologist is familiar with the complexity of cancer mechanisms and with the vast differences between differ-ent types of cancer. Accordingly, it is not surprising when a focused oncologist is unconvinced about the implied link between omega-3 fatty acids and as diverse diseases as cancers, heart attacks, depression, arthritis, and so on. Many special-ists are likely to think that different complex diseases originate from different complex factors, disregarding the possibility of highly beneficial effects of generic and simple answers.

All these specialists would have studied biology and know that all organs consist of biological cells. Of course, different organs consist of differently evolved cells, but the basic cell mechanisms are common. If a specific underlying cause links omega-3 fatty acids with the diverse functions of different organs, it is most likely in the basic cell mechanisms. Various researchers investigated and demonstrated a direct link between consumption of omega-3 fatty acids and ion channels in the cell membrane.[56,57,58,59] The core function of the ion channels is selective transmission of ions into and out of the cell, resulting in charge separation that is analogous to a charged battery. Analogously to charged batteries powering different electronic and mechanical units, adequately charged cells perform different functions, such as the movements of muscles and signal-processing by neurons. With deficiency in omega-3 acids, the cell membrane utilizes omega-6 substitutes, which makes the ion channels far less effective. The retarded cell "batteries" could cause imbalances in some of the more complex mechanisms, depending on specific hereditary and environmental conditions, which then leads to different disorders and diseases.

There could be other links between the observed beneficial effects and omega-3 fatty acids,[60,61] but the specific ion-channel effect relates to proper operation of cells in any organ, any animal, and any human. The flow of ions through the cell membrane is a fundamental mechanism for all cells, so it is no good to think that you could be different because of your continental genes—apparently disconnected from the sea and omega-3 fatty acids in the seafood. *This specific mechanism is general.*

Identifying *specifics with broad implications* is the secret of effective thinking that creates useable and rewarding knowledge.

On the other hand, even the best experts make errors

when they ignore the general implications of specific links. Moreover, we as non-experts can see the errors if the links are simple and we do not ignore them.

Utilize feedback to improve future trials.

A survey of quantum physicists attending one of their conferences found that all participants favored non-statistical and quite bizarre interpretations of quantum mechanics. Nonetheless, most of them could not deny the fundamental quantum randomness of *individual* particles; the majority accepted randomness as a fundamental concept in nature.[62]

Recall how random behavior of individual units turns into a kind of order through the process of trial, error, and occasional but lasting success. This process creates the beauty of crystals from randomly vibrating atoms and—further along the arrow of evolution—it also creates the beauty and complexity of all plants and animals. These are spontaneous processes in chemistry and biology, but humans also create things by random trials. We've used Edison's development of the incandescent lamp as a striking example of similarity with the natural trial-and-error method, so we should use it now to highlight the difference that knowledge and thinking make.

Knowing what to do and how to do it is the meaning of practical knowledge for most people. Some of these people try the same thing over and over again and expect different results, which others like to use as a definition of insanity. Edison's attitude toward knowledge was different. He was recording his failed attempts—thousands of them—and deemed these negative results as knowledge. The following quote displays his attitude toward all these unsuccessful trials: "I have gotten a lot of results! *I know several thousand things that won't work.*"[63] Obviously, we shouldn't waste time and resources by repeating things that didn't work. Knowledge of what already failed is valuable, especially when the failures are someone else's.

As an additional and even more impactful difference, humans use knowledge to improve the chance for success by new trials. Success is not guaranteed, but knowledge makes these trials different from the theorem that a monkey hitting typewriter keys at random is bound to produce meaningful text, given an infinite amount of time.

When writing a new text, humans do use their knowledge. Nonetheless, the first drafts are usually crap. It's usually necessary to analyze the differences between a draft and the desired result and then to revise the text. It's even better if this analysis includes feedback from someone else. Either way, the revision is a new trial that is not based solely on the old knowledge. The new trial utilizes feedback from analyzed differences between the previous draft and the desired result.

If we classify writing as an example of a thinking process, the description of feedback-based revisions is essentially a description of feedback-based thinking loops.

Thinking is a trial-and-error process with feedback. The evolution of cognitive ability to analyze differences from a desired outcome—providing feedback for a new trial—resulted in a quantum leap from the natural selection of purely random trials. Taking wings as an example, we can see a leap from the natural selection of random mutations in birds to the trial-and-error method employed by humans when they attempted to fly. Unlike the termination of unsuccessful random trials by natural selection, humans analyze failed variations of their designs to improve future trials. The quality of this analysis impacts the effectiveness of the feedback and the chance for success by future trials.

However, even the best possible analysis of failed attempts may not find a straightforward path to success. This is not possible when a thinking process has to go through many feedback loops. The following puzzle illustrates this point by showing how multiple loops can get you to the solution of a difficult problem.

Peter and John, mathematicians who graduated from the same University, met each other after many years in a city park. After a few introductory sentences, they engaged in the following conversation about John's children:

Peter: "It's so nice that you also have a boy and a girl! Are they going to school?"

John: "No, still too young."

Peter: "How old are they?"

John: "Have a look at these pigeons; the number you get if you multiply their ages is equal to the number of the pigeons."

Peter: "I see... But that doesn't give me enough information."

John: "Didn't I tell you that my son is older than my daughter?"

Peter: "Oh yes, I know now! Well, they are both younger than my children."

There is enough information in this conversation to work out the ages of John's children. Can you do it?

Clearly, the problem is to work out the children's ages from the text of the puzzle. This leads to the question: What numbers can we get from the text? The first answer is likely to be that the children are younger than six or seven years, depending on the specific school age in John's case. To follow John's hint, we could try multiplications of numbers smaller than 6 or 7. If we do that, we would eliminate multiplications of equal numbers, such as 1x1, 2x2, 3x3, and so on, because we know that one child is older. However, how can this help if we don't know the number of pigeons? There are still many possible options for two different ages below 6 or 7 years that could be multiplied to give the unknown number of pigeons: 1x2, 1x3, 1x4, 1x5, 2x3, 2x4, 2x5, and so on.

At this point, we don't see how we could select only one of all these possible options. However, thinking with feedback loops is not about seeing ahead all the way to the conclusion, but making one step at a time and analyzing the situation before making the next step. Therefore, instead of looking for the solution at this point, we should analyze the failed attempt by multiplying numbers smaller than six or seven while eliminating the multiplications of equal numbers. The key to this analysis is to deal properly with uncertainty and it helps to recall how both Edison and the penicillin team dealt with uncertainty—they searched for new materials not because they knew what material to look for but because there was no knowledge that could rule out successful outcomes. According to this key insight, the uncertainty about possible information that may result from 1x1, 2x2, 3x3, and so on is not a knowledge-based reason to ignore the multiplications of equal numbers. What is relevant is that no knowledge can rule out the possibility that behind the multiplications of equal numbers could be the key to unlock the solution to this problem.

Therefore, we should keep the uncertain information about multiplication of equal numbers and only remove the undoubtedly irrelevant information. That is a proper analysis of the information in this puzzle. We don't know where this will get us, but we may have clearer situation to decide about the next iteration. The following five points summarize the information after removing the irrelevant specifics such as children's gender:

1. John's children are younger than 6 or 7 years.
2. The product of their ages is a number that Peter knows.
3. This number is insufficient information for Peter.

4. The ages of the two children are different.

5. Now, Peter knows the answer.

Following this list, we can see an important change from the insufficient information for Peter (item 3) to Peter knowing the answer (item 5), which had to be caused by the information in item 4 that the ages of the children are different. This means Peter had to eliminate the option that the children are twins.

We begin to see that multiplications of equal numbers is the key for unlocking the solution to this puzzle. Therefore, the next loop should be to identify all different multiplications of two equal numbers as the possible options for the number of pigeons (the number that Peter knows): 1x1=1 pigeon, 2x2=4 pigeons, 3x3=9 pigeons, 4x4=16 pigeons, and so on. Then we should compare any of these options for the number of pigeons to the condition that the ages of the two children are different (item 4). The first option is not good, because the product of two different numbers (children of different ages) cannot be equal to 1. The second option for the number of pigeons is possible, with the ages of the children being 1 year and 4 years (1x4=4 pigeons). The only product of two different numbers that is equal to 9 (the number of pigeons in the third option) is 1x9=9. We rule out this option by the information from item 1 that no multiplying number should be larger than the possible pre-school ages. We can generalize this conclusion to rule out all higher possible products because they involve numbers larger than any pre-school age: 2x8=16, 1x16=16, 1x25=25, and so on. Therefore, the only possible specific solution, consistent with all specific and relevant items of information, is that the children are 1 and 4 years old.

Think positively about negative feedback.

In this puzzle about children's ages, the insight that multiplications of equal numbers was the way toward the solution initiated a sequence of so-called positive-feedback loops. The first was the easy multiplication of two equal numbers as the options for the number of pigeons, which was followed by loops that eliminated all options inconsistent with the remaining information in the puzzle. In general, it's easy to deal with positive feedback—you don't change what works and the progress you are making will continue.

In contrast, negative feedback is far more difficult and the puzzle with children's ages can illustrate the most important element of this difficulty. Negative feedback is inherently linked to a failure or an error, such as the failed initial trial to solve the puzzle by eliminating multiplications of equal numbers because the children's ages were different. This failure did cause negative emotions at that point, but the negative emotions only lasted for as long as we didn't know what to do differently. Not knowing what to change is the real difficulty with negative feedback, which doesn't exist in the doing-more-of-the-same response to positive feedback.

To stress this key point again, the thinking way out of such difficulty is not about seeing a certain path to the final aim but rather analyzing the unsatisfactory situation to find what to try next. If you are an employee and you receive negative feedback, the real difficulty will last only for as long as you don't know what to change. When your supervisor delivers negative feedback with explanations why and what to do differently, it's a relatively easy situation if your thinking is in agreement with the supervisor's assessment. The problem becomes real if your analysis is different, and we will deal with this conflict in the forthcoming chapters.

At this stage, it's helpful to consider the effects of a strong negative feedback. A technical implementation of negative feedback, such as temperature control, provides a good example for this purpose. Negative feedback controls a room temperature by sensing the temperature to trigger an automatic action if the temperature is not changing in the right direction. The controller will either turn the heaters *on* if the temperature is dropping below or turn the heaters *off* if the temperature is increasing above the desired level. These negative-feedback actions reverse temperature departures from the desired level and, in that way, stabilize the temperature. In general terms, negative-feedback actions reverse sensed error signals to keep a system at predetermined parameters.

If you are a manager, or a teacher, or a parent, the strength of the negative feedback—delivered with a request for specific changes—should not be stronger than your conviction in the rightness of what you want to achieve. The temperature-control example shows that the aim of strong negative feedback is to stabilize a system to predetermined parameters. This should not be your aim if you are not confident that differences from your views constitute errors.

Perhaps surprisingly, you should also be cautious when giving positive feedback, and the reason is this: Positive feedback reinforces existing actions, and if they deviate somewhat from the right direction, the deviation will grow and may turn into a disaster. Think how a car turns to the right when you turn the steering wheel to the right. The positive-feedback action is to continue turning the steering wheel to the right, which is good if the car needs to turn further but it becomes a disaster if the road is straight.

This takes us to the point when we need to discuss the *knowledge* that we use to decide what changes to classify as errors for actions by negative feedback, what changes to embrace with positive feedback, and what changes to ignore as irrelevant.

6

Learn from Others but Use the Knowledge Prudently

The nervous system of fish is simple, but a fish still knows whether to jet away from a predator or to jump onto a wiggly worm in response to sensed water vibrations. The water vibrations create electric pulses in a fish's sensory neurons, which travel through synaptic links between its neurons to trigger the adequate muscle action. The role of synapses is to guide the electric pulses to the right muscles, something like memorized phone numbers transmitting your call to one person when you type one number and to another person when you type another number.

Different from the 100 percent replicability of typed phone numbers, water vibrations from predators are never the same. To deal with this variability, the similarity threshold for action is below the perfect 100-percent match between new signals and the synaptic templates. This tricky threshold function is also the key feature of all our decisions. If you see the phrase "add a cup of sguar" in a cooking recipe, you will immediately decide that "sguar" is misspelled "sugar." There is no better match to other words in your memory and the similarity is sufficiently high. This is James's "associative wisdom" and Kahneman's "fast thinking", which Gladwell refers to by the catch phrase "thinking without thinking." [64] Using a more formal term, Leonard Mlodinow, the author of *Subliminal*, calls it "subliminal processing." [65] All these different phrases indicate similarity-based decisions by our automatic system of the brain, described by Thaler and Sunstein in the following way:

> The Automatic System is rapid and is or feels instinctive, and it does not involve what we usually associate with the word *thinking*. When you duck because a ball is thrown at you unexpectedly, or get nervous when your airplane hits turbulence, or smile when you see a cute puppy, you are using your Automatic System. Brain scientists are able to say that the activities of the Automatic System are associated with the oldest parts of the brain, the parts we share with lizards (as well as puppies).[66]

Keep in mind that learning can change the brain "software" but not the "hardware."

William James's "associative paths," which we "share in common with the beasts," consist of neurons and synapses in the automatic system of the brain. A fish inherits associative paths that guide electric signals from its sensors to trigger corresponding muscle actions. This inherited knowledge is essential because learning by trial and error to distinguish predators from wiggly worms is not a feasible survival option for the fish.

Humans also inherit associative paths that enable instinctive actions, such as the sucking instinct in babies and the reflex to snatch a hand away from a hot surface. In fact, we inherit the genetic code for the complete structure of neural networks that constitute the signal-processing "hardware" of our brains. In this analogy, you are born as a set model of a smartphone or a computer, memorizing personalized software as you change synaptic links between your neurons. These synaptic links are analogous to software because they can strengthen or weaken over time due to increased or decreased activity.[67] Neuroscientists use the term "synaptic plasticity" for this effect. Analogously to setting apps in a new smartphone, the growth of synaptic links is very intensive in the first years of a child's life, as the child learns new skills, explores the world, and develops unique personality. When we learn as adults, we are still changing some synaptic links, although it takes more repetitive actions and stronger reinforcement to embed the new knowledge.

When we learn to drive, we establish new associative paths between our eyes and the muscles that slam the brakes when the car ahead of us suddenly stops. In addition to developing *new* synaptic links for automatic actions, we can also change some inherited associative paths. An example is a basketball player who learned to catch a ball thrown at him instead of the instinctive ducking. However, it is very difficult to change some associative paths in the oldest parts of the brain. Although it is possible to learn and become less nervous when your airplane hits a familiar degree of turbulence, you will still get nervous if the airplane hits unexpectedly strong turbulence. It is almost impossible to learn to get nervous when you see a cute puppy and smile when your airplane hits an unexpected turbulence. Therefore, be aware that people can notice when you are nervous and that your colleagues can see whether you are happy, angry, sad, or surprised.

The analogy with different models of smartphones or computers shows that the ability to learn specific skills depends on the set hardware structure of individual brains. It's pointless to upload an app to take high-resolution photos if the smartphone camera is poor. When you read the quote stating that genius is 1 percent talent and 99 percent hard work, remember that the brain hardware determines the talent. Hard work cannot turn a person without musical anatomy into a great singer—an on-key singer, perhaps, but not a great one. Accordingly, innovative people will not do well in jobs that require strict adherence to recipes, whereas people who regard unexpected changes as problems are not the likely innovators.

Of course, an adequate talent is only the essential hardware and substantial effort is necessary to learn advanced skills.

Don't forget that the fundamental learning method is by personal trials, errors, and successes.

You cannot learn to ride a bike just by watching how others do it. You can learn the mechanics of riding, but that falls short of being able to do it.

Rediscovering this fundamental fact, the proponents of experiential learning are dressing it up as a new learning method for the rapid rate of change in the twenty-first century. This new type of learning is supposed to take place without books, without teachers, and without classrooms.

Far from a new phenomenon in the twenty-first century, learning without books, without teachers, and without classrooms predates humanity. Recall how the pigeons learned to make the best choice in the Monty-Hall type puzzle and to maximize their chance for accessing the grain reward. There may have been some communication between the pigeons, but essentially the learning method was by individual trials, errors, and successes. In a similar example, a group of researchers showed that the miniature brain of honeybees, which evolved more than 400 million years before humans, was sufficient to learn by trial and error the basic math operations—addition and subtraction of one unit.[68]

Promoting "experiential learning" as a new method, some of its proponents denigrate the need for teaching as a mere assumption of the twentieth-century education system. However, the need for teaching predates the twentieth century. Our ancestors did not allow their children the freedom to put whatever they liked in their mouth, even though putting objects in the mouth is a common phase of child development. The evolution of communication skills enabled our predecessors to teach their children that some fruits and plants are poisonous. Today's complex knowledge requires more, not less, teaching. Learning without teaching is adequate for the simpler brains of pigeons and honeybees, but it is a step against the arrow of evolution, which is toward increasing complexity. The pigeons with their simple brains did learn to respond to Monty Hall puzzle much faster than humans, but the following joke illustrates a problem with simpler brains:

> Let me tell you, my dear friend, how natural selection deals with sluggishness. For example, we know that a herd of buffalos is as fast as the slowest animal. What happens then is that the herd runs faster when hunters kill the slowest buffalos. The same happens when alcohol tranquillizes the slowest neurons in your brain. That's why, my friend, you speak so much faster when you drink a lot of beer.

Undoubtedly, the slow neurons are not helpful when a driver needs to hit the brake pedal to avoid a fatal crash. However, tranquillizing the slow neurons will not enable the needed fast reaction. What we need instead is to develop fast associative paths that bypass the congestion in the thinking part of the brain.

Developing automatic driving actions does require personal experience, but along with an instructor to avoid fatal learning errors. Learning from personal experience is necessary and most memorable, but the greatness of modern education depends on how well it facilitates learning from *small* errors and, most importantly, from the errors and successes of others. This is the role of teaching.

Be smart to learn from failures and successes of others, but make sure to adapt the knowledge to your situation.

Teaching itself is a good example to illustrate the need for knowledge adaptation to specific scenarios. For many centuries, university professors had been teaching without formal feedback from their students. In that system, professors could teach what they learned from their professors, because there was neither incentive nor real need to evolve their teaching in response to changing environment. University managers had not applied the widespread knowledge about the positive effects of customer feedback until the University of Washington introduced student evaluation of teaching in the 1920s. In the late 1960s and early 1970s, most colleges and universities in North America introduced student evaluation of teaching. Today, the managers in almost all universities in North America and in many countries around the world make use of formal evaluations with numerical student-satisfaction scores as the overall measure.

Numerical satisfaction scores enable managers to rank the employees, or the services, or the products they are evaluating. Customers may provide written feedback and justifications for the given scores in their survey forms, but managers rarely use this feedback to adjust the numerical scores and the consequent ranking. They see the customers' scores as objective numbers that are simple to process and communicate; in contrast, the written feedback requires a time-consuming and potentially subjective analysis. In analogy with the joke about killed buffalos and tranquilized neurons, managers make the evaluation system much faster by eliminating the slow and complex process of feedback analysis. This system works when customers are evaluating products and some, but not all, services. For example, customers can give adequate satisfaction scores for services provided by hotels, airlines, shops, cleaners, gardeners, and so on.

Teaching is different. The knowledge of how to use customer satisfaction scores for performance management *has to be adapted* in the case of teaching to avoid harmful outcomes.

The key difference in the case of teaching is that students cannot make adequate judgment about the quality of teaching before they graduate. The scores that students give to individual courses and professors reflect their satisfaction as they study a particular course. This is different from the satisfaction after they graduate and face evaluation of their own performance. Students see the pain during study, but they see the gain from that pain only after graduation. Of course, university managers can consider *graduated* students as customers who can provide adequate scores for performance evaluation of professors, but this approach is much slower than analyzing the written feedback provided by the students while they are studying.

Management by analysis of students' opinion rather than by mere satisfaction scores has to involve the slowest neurons; when it doesn't, the management system is as simple, as fast, and as good as in the joke about a faster brain when a lot of beer tranquilizes the slow neurons. Some university managers do not use student feedback beyond the satisfaction scores when assessing professors' teaching performance. They consider the students as ordinary customers and adopt management recipes that work for hotel staff and bus drivers. The result is happy students and unhappy graduates.

Do not confuse data with knowledge.

The following exam question would make many engineering students unhappy:

> Two independent electronic units, connected to sensors on an aircraft fuselage, measure the angle of attack (the angle between the airflow and the aircraft's wings). At a certain time instant, the results provided by the first and the second sensor units are 2 degrees and 50 degrees, respectively. What do these results mean?

The answer by many students would be that the average value of the angle of attack is 26 degrees. These students would be unhappy if the professor stated the following as the correct answer:

> The results mean that at least one of the sensing units is providing false data.

The students—and this assumes that none of them is a pilot with the experience to interpret the data in practical terms—would argue that they followed the standard procedure of averaging measurement data to reduce the measurement error. Regarding the unusually large discrepancy between 2 degrees and 50 degrees, the argument would be that they didn't have a criterion for the acceptable discrepancy. Would the professor mark the average value as an incorrect answer if the two measured angles were 2 degrees and 10 degrees? What about 2 degrees and 5 degrees? They would argue that the question was unfairly ambiguous.

As a university manager, you might agree with the students' points. However, you would think differently if you were a passenger, or perhaps even a pilot, on Qantas flight 72 from Singapore to Perth on October 7, 2008. The aircraft was cruising at 37,000 feet in fine and clear weather, until the flight-control computers of the Airbus 330 received the following angle-of-attack data from its sensor units: 2.1 degrees from the first and 50.625 degrees from the second unit, respectively.[69] The computers determined the angle of attack as the average value of 26 degrees—well above the maximum safe value of around 10 degrees—and automatically initiated the maximum nose-down pitch of the aircraft. Many passengers and cabin crew hit the celling as the aircraft dropped down 150 feet in 2 seconds. From the 303 passengers and 12 crew, 119 people suffered injuries at their spines, necks, heads, arms, and legs.

Two minutes before the pitch-down event, the flight-control computers disconnected the autopilot because they received inconsistent data about the aircraft altitude and speed. However, the computers did not give the pilots unfettered control of the flight. Instead, they started sending them brief but frequent over-speed and stall warnings. The captain was Kevin Sullivan, a former US Navy fighter pilot. He realized that something was wrong with the computers because the aircraft could not be flying at both maximum and minimum speeds at the same time. In spite of spitting this inconsistency, the flight computers did not surrender their control and the aircraft continued to fly according to Airbus's normal control law. This meant that the computers allowed the crew to fly the aircraft only within a safe envelope of flight parameters. The angle of attack is one of the parameters that the computers monitor and automatically correct if it exceeds the safe envelope. Two minutes after the flight-control computers disconnected the autopilot, they automatically initiated the maximum nose-down pitch of the aircraft because the average value of 26 degrees was well above the maximum safe number for the angle of attack. Captain Sullivan instinctively pulled back his control stick to thwart the rapid descent, but the computers blocked his action for 2 seconds as the aircraft dropped down 150 feet and injured a third of its occupants.

It took an additional descent of 540 feet during the next 20 seconds before the pilots were able to return the aircraft back to the scheduled altitude of 37,000 feet several minutes later. As they began to respond to numerous warning messages, the aircraft dropped down again. The calculated value of the angle of attack that triggered this second pitch-down event was 16.9 degrees, according to the analysis by Australian Transport Safety Bureau.[70] Their analysis also estimated that the flight crew's control sticks would have had no influence on the aircraft's pitch for about 2.8 seconds. This time the aircraft descended 400 feet over 15 seconds before the flight crew was able to return it to the scheduled altitude.

Three seconds after the second pitch down, the computers disabled the automatic angle-of-attack correction by switching from normal to alternate control law. The alternate control law still didn't give the flight crew full control of the aircraft. For this to happen, the flight-control computers have to decide to switch to Airbus's direct law.

Considering the option for emergency landing at the nearby Royal Australian Air Force base, the captain was worried that he would not be able to stop a pitch down if it happened during landing. However, continuing toward Perth with injured passengers was even riskier. Employing a strategy that Sullivan practiced in fighter jets, the flight crew landed the Airbus 330 at the Air Force base 50 minutes after the first dive.

Sullivan's life and career changed forever. He took eight months off, but when he returned, he could not get rid of the concern about another potential loss of control. A year after Sullivan decided to retire, he opened his heart in an interview for the *Sydney Morning Herald*. Among other statements, he warned against the dark side of automation:

> It is easy to blame the pilots. With all this automation now, "Well, it can't be the aeroplane—it must be the pilot." And in a lot of times it is the pilot, because they're confused. I was certainly confused—we were all confused on that flight. It's a caution sign on the highway of automation to say, "Hey, can you completely remove the human input?"[71]

The Airbus's safety philosophy was not to remove the pilots completely, but to liberate them from uncertainty and, therefore, to enhance safety.[72] Airbus's management introduced this philosophy in the late 1980s, as they decided to take the lead in flight automation. Behind this safety philosophy is the assumption that the source of uncertainty is in the human nature of pilots, whereas the automatic control of aircrafts is completely predictable. To liberate pilots from the uncertainty of their actions, Airbus introduced computer-controlled safety envelope of critical flight parameters. That way, pilots don't need to worry whether they would stall the aircraft by hauling back on the control stick, because the Flight Envelope Protection System will not allow the aircraft to exceed the maximum angle-of-attack number.

Most of the time, the angle-of-attack numbers and all other flight parameters are correct and the protection system works. Consequently, it has made commercial flying easier and a lot safer. This improvement in flight control has been achieved by developing better electronic sensors and by using computers that process volumes of data at speeds and with precision that are unimaginable by humans. Yet, Sullivan's question remains relevant. As soon as he saw the warning messages about the aircraft stalling and over-speeding at the same time, he knew that something was wrong with the data rather than with the actual flight. However, computers do not interpret data to make sense what they mean in reality. In this context, it is insightful to think about the decision of Airbus's management not to allow pilots to take full control of the aircraft until the flight-control computers surrender their envelope protection by switching to the direct control law. This decision implies a much stronger belief in objective data than in humans' ability to interpret reality.

To be fair to Airbus's engineers and management, they did not ignore the fact that measured data are not perfect. That is why they use multiple independent sensors, computers, and software. They also develop algorithms to filter out measurement noise. A forensic analysis by the Australian Transport Safety Bureau showed that the Airbus's algorithms did filter out many spikes in the angle-of-attack data during Qantas flight 72. These spikes were in the form of rapid and short changes from about 2 degrees to the false 50.625 degrees and back to the normal value of about 2 degrees. They were also limited to one of the sensor units. If the pilots could see these spikes, they would undoubtedly interpret them all as noise. In contrast, two specific combinations of these spikes passed through the flight-control algorithm, causing the automatic pitch-down events.

Airbus's decision not to allow the pilots to take full control of the aircraft when they decide to do so has been hotly debated ever since they presented their safety philosophy. An article in the *Science* magazine quotes the following statement by a senior test pilot:

> *Nothing* must have the authority to forbid the pilot to take the actions he needs to. The problem with giving away that authority to a computer is that "a computer

is totally fearless—it doesn't know that it's about to hit something."[73]

Our managers don't like to see us making emotional decisions, so the lack of fear and other emotions may imply that computers can manage critical situations much better. However, as the quoted pilot observed, the lack of fear is because of lack of *knowledge*, which is different from an abundance of data. Electronic sensors can collect data that are more diverse and computers can process them faster than humans can, but an abundance of data cannot replace meaningful knowledge. When the flight-control computers on Qantas's Airbus initiated the rapid nose-down pitch, the pilots felt the upward pressure and saw the blue Indian Ocean in front of them. This was sufficient information to know that the airplane was falling down. Aircraft sensors could collect even more detailed and precise data about the pressure and the image in front of the aircraft, in addition to many more data about the aircraft's situation; however, the flight computers did not have the knowledge to link the data into *awareness* that the aircraft was heading for the Indian Ocean. The flight computers processed the data to send the over-speed and stall warnings, but they did not have the pilot's knowledge to link these messages into the interpretation that something was wrong with the data rather than with the actual flight. The computers did not know that the rapid pitch down injured many passengers. Computers do not know that it may be necessary to break through the safe flight envelope to save passengers even if that action damages the aircraft.

In an apparent failure to learn from smaller errors of others, Boeing introduced a similar automatic correction of the angle of attack on the fourth generation of the most popular aircraft of all time, which they called 737 Max. According to Boeing, the aim was to "deliver improved fuel efficiency and lowest operating costs in single-aisle market."[74] To achieve this aim, they outfitted their 737 Max 8 with bigger and more fuel-efficient engines, but the positioning of those engines increased the potential for the nose to pitch up after take-off.[75] To counteract this risk, Boeing introduced an automated system to push the nose down when its software determines that the sensors are measuring a higher-than-acceptable angle of attack. With this system active, the pilots could no longer take manual control of the plane by simply pulling back on the control stick, as was possible on the older 737s.

Seventeen months after Boeing 737 Max 8 entered service in 2017, it had its first fatal accident, killing all 189 people on board. On October 29, 2018, Lion Air flight JT 610 departed from Jakarta and crashed 12 minutes later into the Java Sea. Less than five months later, on March 10, 2019, Ethiopian Airlines flight ET 302 crashed six minutes after its departure from Addis Ababa, killing all 157 people on board.

Within two days after the crash, more than forty countries around the world grounded all Boeing 737 Max 8 planes. Despite these actions by the safety authorities around the world, Boeing continued to express full confidence in the safety of its 737 Max 8 planes, and even stated that they did not plan to issue new guidance to operators. Ultimately, government regulators and political clout silenced their defense and forced them to take substantive action to solve the problem.

The managers at Boeing had ignored the common-sense point that automatic systems must not be programmed to fight against pilot's actions. This specific knowledge doesn't involve software expertise, but it is sufficient to conclude that computers and automation are the most useful when they work together with people, and under the ultimate authority of the people they are serving. The role of data processed by computers is not to replace but to enhance humans' knowledge. For example, pilots need data from sensors and computers to know their spatial position because, most of the time, they cannot recognize the landscape and the oceans that they see through their windows. Think about the flight-information maps that make not only pilots but also all passengers aware of the aircraft's position.

Knowledge is different from data, and we need both knowledge and data for awareness of the surrounding environment.

Enhance your knowledge to improve your consciousness.

We need more examples for a deeper insight into the relationship between knowledge, data, and awareness of the surrounding environment.

In the first example, Dr. Smith is delivering a presentation about information processing in the human brain. As she makes a strong analogy with data processing in computers, a person from the audience interrupts with the following question: "Are you saying that I am like a programmed machine, without free will? Does this mean that I should not be held responsible if I kill someone?"

"Oh no, certainly not!" Dr. Smith replies almost instantly.

"So, how can your theory be consistent with the concept of free will?"

Dr. Smith stops talking to think about this question. She is aware that describing the brain as a complex computing machine is inconsistent with the concept of free will. She is aware of this conflict and she is thinking about it, however, she is not conscious, meaning that she is not aware of her real environment. That's because she is dreaming. She is not in the seminar room and there is no audience. She did not hear the question she is thinking about. The signals roaming through her brain are unrelated to the real environment.

The next moment, Dr. Smith's hand feels something much softer than a laser pointer. She looks at her hand

and sees that she is in a bed. She looks around and sees an unknown bedroom. The environment she sees is real, but her problem now is that she has no knowledge of the bedroom. Not recognizing the bedroom while realizing that she is not in the seminar room, she still hasn't regained her consciousness.

The next moment, her eyes focus on a coffeemaker that is so common in hotel rooms. This revives her memories of the events before she fell asleep. She remembers her trip to attend a crime-prevention conference, and that she was reading a book about information processing in the human brain while traveling. Now, Dr. Smith can ignore the memories of the presentation about the human brain as a dream and she can ignore the unfamiliarity with details of the room because she rushed into bed shortly after midnight. With this knowledge, she becomes fully aware of her situations and the environment.

Take another example, which is about a driver who fell asleep on the wheel as he was driving a truck full of bags with flour. The truck got off the road on a parking extension and hit a parked vehicle with its side. The crash created a huge cloud of flour, dominating the view in front of the windscreen as it reflected light from the truck's headlights. The driver became aware that he fell asleep while driving and that he'd had an accident. However, the image dominated by the white cloud in front of the windscreen didn't match any of the countless images that he viewed from the cabin of his truck. The idea that what he was seeing could not be the Earth as he knows it, and the awareness of the accident got him to make the following conclusion: "So, I arrived in Heaven with my truck!"

Clearly, after waking up, the driver was conscious of himself inside the truck as the immediate environment. Although this does represent a degree of consciousness, he was not conscious of the fact that he was still alive and on the Earth. The driver believed that his arrival in Heaven was the reason he was seeing the heavenly-looking white stuff, but this match to his imagined Heaven was not a match to knowledge of reality. Consciousness requires knowledge for a *continuous* match—a resonance—with the incoming sensory information. If the knowledge is not realistic, new mismatching information will disrupt the resonance and the apparent awareness will turn into a surprise. In the case of the truck driver, the accumulating information of his environment had to cause a departure from the idea of heaven as the best interpretation of what he was seeing. As the driver inspected the flour bags, the knowledge that the heavenly-looking white stuff was just flour from torn bags provided the lasting explanation. With that knowledge, the degree of his consciousness increased to normal levels. His dissociative experience ended. His usual consciousness took hold again when he had the knowledge to understand the new situation.

The quantity and quality of acquired knowledge determines the degree of consciousness. Long time ago, the knowledge of our ancestors was limited to what they could see on their land. Not knowing what was behind the seas, they developed consciousness of their existence on the Earth as a flat disc surrounded by water. However, some observations of the ancient Greeks did not match that knowledge. After three centuries of trying different ideas by the leading thinkers, they developed the necessary knowledge to make them conscious of the round Earth—but, in the center of the heavens. Then, additional observations disturbed that level of consciousness in some minds, including Nicolaus Copernicus. Today, we fly around the Earth, relying on the level of consciousness reached by the pilots, engineers, and managers in charge of our safety.

Communicate for enhanced consciousness.

Flying is a good example to illustrate how the consciousness of pilots depends on the communication with both instruments and other people. Computers do not interpret data, but they can prepare the data in the form of maps and graphs to enhance the awareness of cockpit crew. Likewise, the interpersonal communication should enhance the awareness of flight controllers. However, this was not so when two Boeing 747s collided at Tenerife's runway on March 27, 1977, in what became the deadliest accident in aviation history.

Both jets—KLM Flight 4805 and Pan Am Flight 1736—were at the small airport on the Spanish island of Tenerife due to interrupted flights. After hours of stopover, the traffic control began maneuvering the jets to position the KLM aircraft for departure. The captain of the KLM flight was Veldhuyzen van Zanten, one of the airline's most respected pilots. He had been the Head of the Flight Training Department and instructor for more than ten years. As it happened, he had certified the license of the first officer sitting next to him in the cockpit. When KLM 4805 turned around at the end of the runway to face in the direction for takeoff, a low-lying cloud was moving toward the aircraft reducing the visibility to below 900 meters. In the past, the runway had always been clear when the air traffic control positioned van Zanten's aircraft for takeoff and, critically, this knowledge removed the uncertainty in his mind that an obstacle might be inside the cloud. He believed the runway was clear, but he was not aware that the Pan Am jet was taxiing toward them. It would've been a very different situation if sensors and computers projected images of the runway on a screen so that the captain could see through the cloud. However, this technology was not available, and the captain had to rely on the radio communication with the traffic controller and with the Pan Am crew to build his mental picture about the reality on the runway.

The traffic controller also had to rely on radio communication to know the positions of the two jets, because he also couldn't see them from the control tower. Knowing that the

Pan Am jet was still taxiing on the runway, the traffic controller didn't give takeoff clearance to the KLM crew. However, believing that the runway was clear, van Zanten was not going to wait for the clearance. He didn't need traffic-control clearances in the training environment that he had been involved in for a long time. According to a post-accident analysis by the Air Line Pilots Association, brain conditioning by the training environment contributed to van Zanten's belief that they were ready for takeoff.[76]

Noticing van Zanten's intention to start the ground run, the first officer told the captain, "Wait a minute, we don't have an ATC clearance." The captain replied, "No, I know that, go ahead, ask." In response, the control tower provided them with instructions for the route after takeoff, which was the ATC clearance, but did not clear them for the takeoff. Following the usual protocol, the first officer was reading back the route instructions when van Zanten started the ground run. Then, the first officer finished his message with tremulous voice and hurried words that sounded like "we are now at takeoff."[77] With his mindset, the traffic controller interpreted the meaning of these ambiguous words as "we are now at takeoff position" and responded by "Okay." It took about two seconds for controller's doubt about this interpretation to grow to the point when he decided to add the following clarification: "Stand by for takeoff ... I will call you."[78]

The KLM crew heard clearly the "Okay" from the controller, but a whistling noise obscured the subsequent request to stand by for takeoff. This whistling noise was due to an overlap with a message from the Pan-Am's co-pilot, who rushed to announce that they were still taxiing down the runway, in response to the words "we are now at takeoff" from the KLM co-pilot and the "Okay" from the flight controller.

The traffic controller heard the Pan Am message that they were still taxiing and instructed them to report when the runway was clear. The Pan Am crew replied, "Okay, will report when we're clear." These messages were audible in the KLM cockpit and the flight engineer, sitting behind the captain, heard them and asked, "Is he not clear, then?" The captain's response was, "What do you say?" and the flight engineer clarified his question, "Is he not clear that Pan American?"[79] At that point, it was still possible to abort the takeoff, but the captain responded with an emphatic "yes" and continued the run.

Captain van Zenten's confidence in his knowledge diminished his ability to hear the warning messages from both the first officer and the flight engineer and, consequently, prevented him from becoming conscious of the real situation on the runway.

Seconds after his emphatic "yes," van Zanten saw the Pan Am in front of them. He immediately pulled back on the control stick to lift the plane off the ground in an attempt to fly over the Pan Am jet, which was turning off the runway in their attempt to avoid the collision. After scraping the runway with its tail, the KLM plane lifted off the ground; its nose and front landing gear cleared the Pan Am fuselage, but its main landing gear hit it. KLM's short flight ended in a sudden and violent fire as it smashed on the ground about 150 meters from the badly damaged Pan Am jet. This crash killed 583 people with only 61 survivors in the front section of the Pan Am aircraft.

Sometimes you have to act on doubt.

Spanish authorities led the formal investigation, with representatives from the Netherlands, the United States, and the two airlines. The Netherlands investigators agreed with the facts and evidence established in the joint investigation. However, their interpretation of the facts and evidence differed substantially from the interpretation in the official report by the Spanish authorities, which blamed the KLM captain for the accident. In response, the Netherlands

Department of Civil Aviation published their interpretation.[80]

One of the points in the Dutch response is about the doubt of the flight engineer, which he demonstrated when he asked whether the Pan Am cleared the runway. The response states that the flight engineer would have taken action to abort the takeoff, for instance by closing the throttles, if he wasn't sure that the runway was clear. It also states that the flight engineer "would have been fully authorized" to take this action "in case of real doubt."

In principle, the logic of the Dutch authorities is correct: We have to act on doubt if the risk of acting is small in comparison to the risk of not acting. In this case, the risk of closing the throttles was insignificant in comparison to the risk of the Pan Am plane taxiing on the runway toward them. The big unanswered question, however, is whether the training of the flight engineer was consistent with this logic.

The prevailing training is not to contradict the actions of our superiors, especially not if we have the opportunity to ask questions and we receive black-and-white answers. But, is this safer in comparison to making free-will decisions based on our own sense of the relevant risks?

7

Think About Risk and Benefit to Make Free-Will Decisions

You do know that Google, Facebook, Microsoft, Apple, Samsung, telephone companies, retailers, governments—and the list goes on—collect your personal information. Analytics companies process these data by sophisticated algorithms and assert that they can predict what you and others will buy in the future. For example, the web pages of one of the largest database marketing companies, Acxiom, state that their advanced analytics "accurately predict consumer brand affinity and preferences, in-market interests and timing, and media viewing habits."[81]

It's good for everyone when these predictions enable personalized marketing to deliver the right information to individual consumers. However, we all know that the efficiency of this method is far from 100 percent, and the interesting question is what to do with the errors. The slippery logic here is to disregard the prediction errors as no more than noise due to random decisions of some consumers. Consequently, this logic leads to what appears as the only other alternative—focus on the non-random, hence predictable, decision-making.

The view that it's possible to predict and even control the behavior of others—unless they are freaks—contradicts what we feel as our free will when making personal decisions. Free will has been an insurmountable concept for scientists and philosophers. The only possible options they see are deterministic and random actions, and neither of them is consistent with the concept of free will. Disregarding it as a philosophical problem and confused by science, many decision makers succumb to the predictability promised by analytics and fueled by ever-increasing data collection.

This trend means that people will be less motivated to talk to you and more interested to shove down your throat what their analytics tell them, and if you don't buy it, they will abandon you as a freak. What's even worse, you cannot even conceive the wrong profiles and judgments that algorithms will make about you when they get it wrong. We should stay away from this dangerous cliff as we all follow the road that big data and analytics are tracing for us. That's why, in this chapter, we'd like you to take a look at the concept of free will beyond the black-and-white picture of either predictable or random actions.

Don't accept the logic that purely random choices are the only alternative to predictable decisions.

The following simple example can illustrate why seeing only two alternatives—either purely random choices or predictable decisions—is a view through a black-and-white filter. It's a simple example, but it relates to the most difficult concept in philosophy and science—your freedom and ability to make unpredictable and yet non-random decisions by *learning and thinking.*

A friend used to buy refined vegetable oil for many years. One day, she heard somewhere that some oils oxidize when exposed to heat, resulting in harmful compounds. Thinking and reading more about this effect, she found that the refining process heats the oils to a much higher temperature than normal cooking. No analytics algorithm could've predicted it, but she stopped buying refined oil.

When our friend heard about the oxidation of oils, she decided to learn more about its effects. However, there was no set science and no uniform expert advice to determine her subsequent action. Because of this uncertainty, her response was different from what many others would've decided.

To begin with, she didn't take the easiest option to dismiss the new information as a marketing ploy for the competing virgin oils.

The next option was to trust the experts recommending refined oils for frying and virgin oils for salad dressing. These experts explain that frying temperatures exceed the smoke point of most virgin oils, releasing harmful free radicals as the oil burns. On the other hand, the refining process increases the smoke point and these oils remain stable during frying. Like many others, our friend could've adopted this advice.

However, she continued to read, learn, and think. Eventually, she found that the smoke point of high-quality extra-virgin olive oil is higher than the usual frying temperature. With this information, she decided it was safer to cook with virgin olive oil. She acted on her doubt about the effects of the much higher temperatures used during the refining process.

This was neither random nor predictable decision. What makes this a free-will decision is the learning and thinking that our friend employed to assess the risks and benefits of the available options.

Think beyond data to make free-will decisions.

You may or may not be able to imagine yourself as a real-estate agent, but anyone could try the simple job in the following thought experiment. Consider a real-estate agency with a huge database and powerful analytics able to accurately match potential buyers and available properties. Your job in this agency is to show a buyer a few houses that match her profile in the database. That's all you need to do.

The first property you show is a great value with an excellent resale potential. It's a typical house in a sought-after location. After the inspection, the buyer tells you she wants to change her lifestyle by transitioning to retirement. She would like a house with distinct features and with a socializing potential. This change in the buyer's situation ramps up the risk that she will not like the remaining properties on the analytics list.

A free-will action would be to reduce the risk for yet another negative response by changing the plan and showing different houses. However, without information about other available properties, you cannot exercise your free will. Furthermore, a mere access to the agency's database is not sufficient, because you need the expertise of a real-estate agent. In other words, you need knowledge that is different from mere data. Without this knowledge, your choice of different houses would be a random trial and, in analogy with a decision by coin tossing, this would not be a free-will decision.

On the other hand, with knowledge and ability to analyze the new information provided by the buyer in the context of her profile in the database, you can begin to shape a new idea about the next house you could try. This is the thinking process, which forms feedback from your analysis of the failed attempt to a better subsequent trial. In this example, the thinking process would involve a constructive conversation with the buyer, trying not only to meet her needs but also to help her specify the desired distinctive features.

Make free-will decisions today for favorable automatic actions in the future.

Knowledge also plays a key role in scenarios when there is no time for learning and thinking, hence no time for risk assessment to make free-will decisions. In the absence of adequate knowledge, random actions are the only available option in these scenarios—think of a twitching fish out of water. In contrast, proper knowledge makes a big difference as it triggers the right automatic actions. A good example is driving knowledge, which ensures that you stomp on the brake pedal when the car in front of you suddenly stops. This automatic action occurs before you become conscious of the changing situation and, consequently, it is not a free-will action.

The outcomes of driving exams are either pass or fail. There is no gray area and—in an ideal world—there is no need for risk assessments and free-will decisions; only drivers with licenses, attesting adequate driving knowledge, are on the road. However, gray areas do exist in the real world. Assume that person X has a valid driving license but, for some reason, hasn't been able to drive for several years after the driving exam. One evening, he is under the peer pressure to drive a friend's car after a party where, unlike person X, most others had quite a few drinks.

The decision not to drive would be a free-will choice in this circumstance. Saying "no" to a risky demand is a sure sign of free will. If you say "no" when your supervisor asks you to perform a task you don't think you should do, you are exercising your free will. The key element here is your thinking. Whether you say "yes" or "no," the engagement of your reflective system to think and analyze gray scenarios distinguishes free-will decisions from both automatic and random actions. If you don't bother to think and just do what you are told to do, you are abandoning your free will. On the other hand, saying "yes" *is* a free-will choice when thinking makes you aware of the involved risk. In the example of person X, he is aware of the risk that his driving experience may not be adequate for the highway traffic that's awaiting the group. Therefore, his choice to take the driving risk rather than the risk of resisting the peer pressure is a free-will decision.

Once they are on the busy highway, a car in front of them suddenly stops. Instead of pressing on the brake pedal, the subconscious action of person X is to move away from the stopping car by turning suddenly into the adjacent lane. The next moment, they hit another car in the adjacent lane, which causes sliding of both cars and piling up of additional vehicles into a tragic accident.

The situation where the car ahead of them suddenly stopped, instead of cruising at the highway speed, was a new situation for person X. He did not have the time to think and to assess properly the risks of the available options. He was not conscious of the fact that the turn into the adjacent lane would cause an accident.

Philosophers use similar examples to argue that free will cannot exist. Their argument considers both predetermined and random actions as two black-and-white scenarios. In the deterministic scenario, the sight of the brake light creates neural signals in the eyes of person X, and those signals then travel through his neurons and synapses to the arm muscles turning the steering wheel. The argument is that this is not different from a programmed robot and electrical signals travelling from its sensors to the actuators.

The other alternative is a random flow of neural signals to the arm muscles. Person X is not a hard-wired robot, so this is what's happened in his neural system. The reason is the absence of adequately trained synaptic links to take the signals to the leg muscles for pressing on the brake pedal.

Either way, many philosophers conclude that free will cannot exist because there is neither "freedom" in the deterministic option nor "will" in the random option, and no other option exists in their black-and-white view. The belief that nothing else is possible beyond this neither-nor logic has significant implications. For example, punishing sinners and criminals is a flawed concept of justice according to the true believers in the absence of free will.

Disregarding this philosophical view, our society maintains justice system with punishment of people who break established rules. In the example of person X, the necessary investigation will conclude that he did not follow the driving rules and punishment will follow. Turning the car into the adjacent lane was a subconscious action, but that's not all that matters. What is also important here is the conscious decision to drive without the knowledge needed for automatic actions in compliance with the driving rules. Person X was aware of the driving risk, but he decided to drive because resisting the peer pressure seemed like a bigger risk. This risk analysis turned out to be flawed but, as a distinguishing feature of free will, it was neither random nor predetermined. With a better risk analysis, person X would've decided not to drive.

Punishment by the justice system will help person X learn a lesson not to take the same risk again, leaving him with two options: either don't drive again or renew your training by taking driving lessons. Selecting between these options, it would be a free-will decision to drive with an instructor and to consolidate his driving knowledge. When driving in the future with better trained synapses, not only pressing on the brake pedal but also many other actions will be automatic; however, it's wrong to argue that these automatic actions have nothing to do with his free will and with the related responsibility for his decisions. All these automatic actions will relate back to the free-will decision to acquire adequate driving knowledge.

This example shows that knowledge does *determine* some future actions, but it also shows that much of our knowledge results from our free-will decisions what to learn and how much to learn. Therefore, don't engage with the black-and-white view that your future actions can be only either determined or random and, accordingly, you have no free will to change them. Don't allow these experts to infest you with a doubt in your free will. Focus on your ability to learn, think, and make decisions according to your own vision and judgment.

Don't take a long-term risk for a short-term benefit.

Person X took the unnecessary risk to drive because of peer pressure. Taking unnecessary risks is common in the business world, and the usual reason is competitive pressure. An excellent example is the situation that lured Boeing to launch the flawed 737 Max version of its most popular airplane.

Recall the discussion about automation as a method to prevent pilots from taking actions outside a known envelope of safe flying parameters. Airbus championed this philosophy as their modern and superior approach to safety. In contrast, Boeing's safety philosophy was to keep pilots in control of the planes as much as possible. Many pilots preferred this approach, some of them saying, "If it's not Boeing, I'm not going."[82] All this changed unexpectedly after Boeing's decision to develop the 737 Max. The result of this change is 346 dead people, killed in two crashes less than six months apart, when the pilots of Ethiopian Airlines and Indonesia's Lion Air couldn't counteract the newly introduced automatic pitch-down of these airplanes.

Nobody in Boeing and nobody in the Federal Aviation Administration (FAA) wanted to make a decision that would contribute to an airplane crash. It happened in the environment of an increasing competition from A320neo—a plane that Airbus announced in 2010 to reduce the cost of flying. Airbus's engineers upgraded the older A320 models with bigger engines, which is the most effective way of improving the fuel efficiency of an airplane. Boeing also used this method in the past when they increased the engine size while maintaining the airframe of their original 737 model, introduced as far back as 1967. You may have noticed that the shape of engines in 737's is oval, which is the trick that the engineers in Boeing used to fit them in the limited space under the wings. However, Airbus 320 could accommodate even bigger engines in the A320neo model, whereas there was no space under the wings of the old 737 airframe to match the efficiency of the Airbus's new model.

Initially, Boeing's management dismissed the emerging threat from A320neo and did not initiate the development of a new more efficient aircraft with a new airframe to fit bigger engines. However, this attitude suddenly changed in 2011 when the chief executive of American Airlines—an exclusive Boeing customer for many years—surprised Boeing's leadership by telling them that American Airlines were poised to place an order for hundreds of Airbus's fuel-efficient jets. In this unexpected situation, one option for Boeing executives was to manage the loss of revenue and to focus on the future development of new competitive airplanes. In other words, lose the battle to focus on winning the war. However, they decided to match the competing fuel efficiency of A320neo by doing whatever was necessary to upgrade the existing 737 model with larger engines. In addition, they decided to limit all other changes so that they could present the new 737 Max version as essentially the same as earlier 737 models. That way, they could get a quick certification by the FAA, saving valuable time. They would also avoid the requirement for pilot training in a flight simulator, cutting down cost for airlines.

To fit a larger engine under the wing of the old 737 airframe, the solution was to move the engine up, which could be achieved by extending it well in front of the wing. However, the shifted engines acted as wing extensions, creating an undesirable lift in front of the wings. This was a serious problem when the aircraft was climbing and the angle between the wings and the airflow—the angle of attack— was high. According to Gregory Travis, a pilot for thirty years and a developer of aviation software, the additional lift could increase a high angle of attack even further, and possibly so much that the pressure under the wings would no longer be sufficient to keep the aircraft in the air. This is a fatal scenario when the wings lose their function and the aircraft falls down in what is called an aerodynamic stall. Travis described this design as "aerodynamic malpractice of the worst kind."[83]

However, the focus of Boeing's executives was to minimize the imminent loss of revenue to their competitor. With this mindset, they decided to solve the problem with an automatic anti-stall system. This seemingly simple system would sense the angle of attack and, if the angle increases toward the dangerous stall level, the flight computer would automatically tilt the little wings on the horizontal tail to pitch down the aircraft. They developed the automatic system under the obscure name "Maneuvering Characteristics Augmentation System," or MCAS. The "decision maker" in this system was a software code, which in its final version used the data from a single angle-of-attack sensor.

It remains unclear why the final design was a system that could crash an airplane due to a failure of a single sensor. According to a report in *The New York Times*, Boeing engineers did analyse the risk of MCAS activation if the sensor fails, and the conclusion was that this could happen less often than once in 10 million flight hours.[84] This number means an erroneous triggering of MCAS could occur every year with

5,000 airplanes flying on average six hours a day. Of course, nobody in Boeing would accept the chance that their airplanes would crash every year, so it seems they didn't consider the events of false MCAS activation as fatal. In other words, it seems they took the risk of dealing with the issue of angle-of-attack sensor as a single point of failure once the 737 Max is in operation and when MCAS malfunction occurs.

To adhere to its safety principle of keeping pilots in control of the planes as much as possible, 737 Max pilots would have needed to be trained on a simulator to know how to use the new anti-stall system and, importantly, how to take control of the aircraft when they decide to disable it. That would have increased costs and lengthened the certification process by the FAA. Instead, Boeing asked senior FAA officials whether it would be okay to remove MCAS from the pilot's manual, and the FAA approved this request. It is a surprising decision by the aircraft certification body, whose touchstone value is integrity: "We perform our duties honestly, with moral soundness, and with the highest level of ethics."[85] The chairperson of the House Transportation Committee, Rep. Peter A. DeFazio (D-OR), referred to this approval by the following words during a House oversight hearing: "So how could the FAA agree to that? Did they understand what it did? Did anybody understand what this would do? I don't think the implications were fully known."[86]

DeFazio's conclusion that the FAA officials did not know the implications of their decision is an example of what is known as Hanlon's razor: "Never attribute to malice that which is adequately explained by stupidity."[87,88]

Nobody can attribute the decisions by both Boeing and the FAA to malice; that's beyond any doubt. However, to accept a lack of knowledge, or ignorance, or incompetence, or stupidity as the only other alternative is to assume that the professionals in Boeing and FAA make their decisions without thinking and without risk analyses. This is not so, because they are not programmed robots and they don't leave their free wills at home as they head to work. They did think and they did perform risk analyses, so the real question here is this: What did they think about? The FAA's mission "to provide the safest, most efficient aerospace system in the world" suggests that they thought about the safety of passengers and crew, but also about the efficiency of aerospace system. This brings us to the key question: Was the efficiency of aerospace system improved by the decision not to tell the airlines about MCAS and, consequently, to save them millions of dollars by avoiding the need to train their pilots in a simulator?

The answer is "yes" if we assume that a fast and inexpensive certification process was the specific meaning of "efficiency" for the FAA officials. After all, even the most elaborate certification process could not reduce to zero the risk that something could go wrong. There is no alternative to the trial-and-error method: Let the airplanes fly and, when something doesn't work as expected, analyze the event and make changes to improve the safety of aerospace system. Related to the specific MCAS case, the FAA determined that—if something went wrong and MCAS mistakenly started forcing the plane's nose downward—pilots would recognize this behavior as a *general issue* with the wings on the horizontal tail. The implication is that pilots didn't need training and didn't even need to know about MCAS. According to an explanation by the FAA, the existing "emergency procedure for which pilots are trained will stop the action of MCAS."[89] This clearly shows that FAA officials thought about the risk they are taking by not including MCAS in the pilot's manual. They concluded the risk was manageable. The benefit was a highly efficient certification process, which enabled Boeing to start selling the new airplanes without certification delays and without the expensive pilot training.

However, the FAA's classification of possible MCAS malfunction as a "general issue" should ring the alarm bells for anyone who knows that generalizations ignore specifics. When MCAS pitched down the nose of Lion Air, it also automatically pushed the pilot's control column forward. The pilots did not see this as a general issue with the tail wings and instead pulled the control column back to lift the nose up, which they could do as soon as MCAS force stopped. The tragic accident would not have happened if MCAS did not activate repeatedly after the pilots corrected its action. Unfortunately, MCAS was not programmed to allow the pilots to take control and the airplane crashed into the Java Sea killing everyone on board. Realizing that the Lion-Air pilots didn't switch off the power to the tail wings, Boeing decided to issue a specific instruction to all pilots to do so if MCAS mistakenly begins to pitch down the airplane. Less than six months later, the pilots of the Ethiopian Airlines did that, but it did not help, and they turned the power on again in their futile attempt to stop the tragic dive and to pull up the airplane.

A question related to the efficiency of the FAA certification is whether they could have done something to avoid these experiments with real lives, and the answer is "yes." These days, pilots can run trial-and-error experiments in a flight simulator. However, Boeing didn't test the MCAS operation in a flight simulator and the FAA didn't ask them to do it. Taking the risk of not doing it, they saved time and money. It's now painfully obvious that the short-term efficiency of the certification process ended up—in the longer term—tragically inefficient in terms of safety and financially inefficient for Boeing.

A lesson we can all learn from Boeing's example is this: If losing a battle will not kill you, do not try to win it by taking deadly risks.

Don't think that sharing personal responsibilities will reduce risk.

The close relationship between Boeing and the FAA is a good example of an increased risk when a teamwork dilutes personal responsibilities. The closeness of this relationship evolved as FAA engineers migrated to better-paid jobs at Boeing. With increasing complexity of airplanes and dwindling number of skilled engineers, the FAA was no longer able to assess the safety of new airplanes independently. To deal with this problem, they introduced the concept of "design engineering representatives" (DERs)—people employed by airplane manufacturers who had to certify to the FAA that their designs were safe.

The interest of both the manufacturers and the FAA is that the airplanes are safe, so it makes sense if they work as a team and utilize the best available experts to achieve this common aim. However, the FAA increased the risk of certifying unsafe designs by sharing with DERs their responsibility for safety. This is because safety was not the primary responsibility of DERs. They worked under Boeing management and their primary job was to deliver 737 Max as soon as possible and to avoid the need for additional training of 737 pilots. These constraints imposed limits to their safety considerations. They had to implement the automatic anti-stall system. DERs were not brave enough to tell the management that—if an accident occurred—external experts could regard the software fix of the aerodynamic instability as a malpractice. On the other hand, the feeling of personal protection in the Boeing Company resulted in a lack of fear from the FAA and, consequently, caused the DERs to underestimate the risk of malfunction by their designs. Just like other companies, Boeing can provide a degree of protection to its employees, including criminal investigations, but it cannot guarantee that the authorities will not prosecute individuals.

You are responsible for your free-will decisions even when you work as a team member. Furthermore, the individual decisions of all members in a holistically organized group are just as important as the decisions by the group leader. The story of a young Australian cricketer will encourage you to say "no" to protect the whole team, including your leader.

In Australia and in many other countries of the former British Empire, cricket is a national sport of utmost importance. A former Prime Minister of Australia used to joke that he had the second most important job in the country, the most important leader being the captain of the national cricket team. This most responsible role belonged to Steven Smith when Australia was playing South Africa in March 2018. The match was slipping away as the Aussies could not get the ball past South Africa's batsmen. This drove the leadership group, including the captain Steven Smith and the vice-captain David Warner, to come up with the idea of roughening up the ball by sandpaper in a hope that this would create a helpful reverse swing. They discussed this illegal ball tampering during a break in play. Warner instructed the team's youngest member, Cameron Bancroft, to carry out their plan. Bancroft had developed a strong reputation that he was willing to do whatever he could to help the team. He was motivated to maintain the benefit of this reputation. In his own words, Bancroft didn't think he was coerced to do it. He was nervous about his new role because there were hundreds of cameras around; he was aware of the risk but he decided to take it.

Once on the field, a camera caught Bancroft's action of taking sandpaper out of his pocket and rubbing the ball. When he realized that he was sighted on the screen, Bancroft stuffed the sandpaper down his pants in panic. When the empire approached him, he attempted to hide the evidence by showing a piece of cloth in his pocket.

They lost the match, but the worst was yet to come.

Following an investigation, the Cricked Australia Board charged Smith, Warner, and Bancroft with a breach of the Code of Conduct. The Board suspended them from all international and domestic cricket, Bancroft for nine months and Smith and Warner for 12 months. They also had to undertake 100 hours of voluntary service in community cricket and lost sponsorship deals.

Bancroft was aware that ball tampering in front of so many cameras was very risky and, on his own, he probably wouldn't make the decision to do it. The benefit of possible turn around in the match was too small to take the risk. However, a big factor in his decision was that the instruction to do it came from his vice-captain. Enhancing his reputation as a responsive team player was an additional benefit for Bancroft. On the other hand, to say "no" required a mental effort to make a big-picture analysis and to tell his superiors that the risk was unreasonable. These discussions were happening during lunch break, so he had some time to think about the instruction and to act in a way that not only would reflect a stronger free will but also would be beneficial well after the match they were plying.

Distinguish single occurrences from repeated events when assessing risk.

Our emphasis on assessing risk and making decisions from your own perspective is different from what economists tell us about rational behavior. A representative example is the economic theory that rational people *should* choose the option with the highest "expected utility." Two psychologists, Daniel Kahneman and Amon Tversky, conducted many experiments and showed that the expected-utility theory doesn't predict people's behavior.[90,91] We will use here a set of numbers from their experiments to show why people's choices differ from scientific models, such as the expected-utility theory.

The crux is in the meaning of "expected utility," so we will use a realistic example rather than abstract numbers to explain it. In the example, we consider a new retail shop and an idea of its management to promote it by offering free vouchers to a random selection of one hundred shoppers. To make it more engaging, the management decides to offer each of these hundred shoppers two options: (1) take a $400 voucher or (2) play a game with 50-percent chance to win a $1,000 voucher and 50-percent chance to miss out. Assuming that these dollar values represent the actual utilities for all hundred customers, the expected utility for option 2 is $500. It is calculated as a half of $1,000 to account for the 50-percent chance of winning. This value is higher than the $400 in option 1 and, according to the expected-utility theory, all rational customers should select option 2.

The question you should ask here is about the meaning of $500, given that the available vouchers are only for $400 and $1,000. Recall the metaphor that you are buying a pig in a poke if you relay on data without checking their interpretation. The interpretation in this case is that the expected utility of $500 is the *average* win per participant taking option 2. If all participants select option 2, the expected win by the whole group is 50 vouchers with the total value of $50,000, which gives the average of $500 per participant. But, why does this average matter?

The answer is that economic theories use the certainty of averages instead of bothering with the uncertainty of individual events. In this example, the expected-utility concept is not about the 50 percent chance as the uncertainty for a win or a loss by a specific participant; instead, its exclusive focus is on the certainty that the average win in option 2 is around $500. Analogously to exact sciences, economic theories assume that the law of large numbers can filter out erratic behavior of individuals to represent the rational decisions of an average consumer.

To be fair, the use of average values is necessary and quite common. For example, if you read that the Food and Drug Administration recommends taking 78 grams of fat a day, you know that these are 78 grams *on average* and for an average person. Still, this is a very useful quantitative information when compared to the recommended 50 grams of protein a day, especially if you've been trying to avoid fat at all cost. Nonetheless, the use of averages can be misleading. For example, comparing the wealth between nations, *The Global Wealth Report 2018* by Credit Suisse Research Institute shows that the average wealth of adults in US is about $400,000. This is lower than the average of $530,000 in Switzerland but much higher than Brazil's average of less than $17,000. The implication from these averages that Americans are wealthier than Brazilians is misleading—the wealth of more than a quarter of American adults is below $10,000 and many of them are actually in debt. Economic theories dealing with averages ignore the fact that people in debt are not thinking how to increase the average wealth. Furthermore, these people are not irrational when they make decisions to improve their individual situations, even if this reduces the average number.

Likewise, the average of $500 in the example with vouchers doesn't mean much to the individual participants. The concept of expected utility is meaningless from the perspective of an individual. A rational person could clearly see that the average value of $500 is not a wining option. Instead, the meaningful options are the certainty of $400 and the 50-percent chance to either miss out or win $1,000. Cashing the luck of $400, in preference to the 50-percent chance of losing, is a very sensible choice. Still, this doesn't mean it's irrational if someone gives away the luck of $400 for the chance to win $1,000. It would be irrational if that person believed he or she was destined to win the game. However, it's a rational free-will decision if the person is conscious of the risk and wants to play the game for the fun of it.

The experiments conducted by Kahneman and Tversky showed that the majority of people—but not everyone—choose the certainty of $400. These results are consistent with rational decisions of individuals who don't care about the average win by the whole group of hundred people.

The following example can show what makes scientists conclude that the theory is sound, whereas people are irrational. Recall how two scientists trained pigeons to make favorable decisions in the Monty-Hall problem. Applying the trial-and-error method of training pigeons to the example with vouchers, the birds would have the choice of 400 grains every time they peck a key for option 1 and, with the chance of 50 percent, they would get 1,000 grains if they peck an alternative key representing option 2. After a lengthy trial-and-error series, the pigeons would learn that getting 1,000 grains with the chance of 50 percent—the utility of 500 grains on average—is the better option. Different from people's preference for option 1, this is in agreement with the expected-utility theory.

Consider now the example when you also have the opportunity to make not one but repeated choices between the certainty of $400 and 50-percent chance for $1,000. If you are allowed to do this a hundred times, no doubt you would select the 50-percent chance for $1,000 every single time. The law of large numbers works because the actual two options now are either the certainty to collect the total of $40,000 or the expected total win of $50,000. A comparison between these sums would be the basis for your decisions but, theoretically, your average win of $500 per each of the hundred trials is in agreement with the expected-utility theory.

What is happening here is that this example is different from the scenario of one bite at a cherry, and this difference is the crux of the problem with the theory.

A trained pigeon would go for option 2 even if—days

after training—the conditions change from repeated opportunities to only one chance to peck one of the two keys. This behavior would be like robots programmed to always select the option with the highest expected utility. Neither pigeons nor programmed robots can comprehend the uncertainty associated with a 50-percent chance in a one-off opportunity. Humans can, and with this awareness comes the ability to think and make free-will decisions whether to take the certainty of $400 or to have fun with option 2. The bottom-line is that, just as trained pigeons and programmed robots lack this awareness and ability to think, the expected-utility theory ignores the ability of humans to make free-will decisions.

What this example shows is that we should consider the free will of others if we wish to make the right judgment about their behavior.

Moreover, rather than labeling people as irrational, the example shows that taking into account the free will of consumers can lead to more profitable business decisions. To see how this works on the example with vouchers, assume that 80 people take the $400 option and ten of the remaining 20 participants are lucky and win $1,000 vouchers. This scenario is better for the shop managers who'd spend less money to make more customers happy; they would give away $42,000 to 90 people, as distinct from the expected-utility solution of $50,000 given to 50 lucky winners.

An even better example for the positive effects of free-will decisions is the insurance business. According to the expected-utility theory, a chance of one in a thousand to claim a house damage of $500,000 corresponds to the premium of $500. However, if the insured customers do not pay more than the expected loss, there is neither money for admin costs nor profit for the insurance business. The question then is why people pay more so that the insurance companies are able to cover admin cost and make profit.

From the perspective of an insured individual, the question why pay more than $500 in this example is not the right question. If this is a yearly premium, the chance of one in thousand to make a claim means that the expected time to make that claim is 1,000 years! Clearly, people don't pay insurance premiums with the expectation to get the money back. When paying for insurance, people make the free-will decision to lose the paid premium. They pay if they can afford the premium and don't want to risk even the small probability of one in thousand to lose $500,000. From this perspective, it is not a big difference to pay either $500 or $700 per year. Yet, paying more than the expected loss enables insurance companies to operate.

Looking at the insurance business in positive light, the group of insured people are helping one another. The premium payments are small enough so not to hurt badly when the insured people pay them, but they save a small number of unlucky people from the devastating losses of insured properties. This is a simple example of how people can make up for bad luck by forming groups. However, forming groups and working in teams to minimize risk is a far bigger deal with profound effects.

PART C

The Emotional-Intelligence Level

8

Minimize Risk and Maximize Opportunities by Working in Holistic Teams

For all but the most altruistic, we invest personal effort in teamwork for our own benefit—no personal benefit, no teamwork.

Take the example of a group of experts whose task is to solve an elusive problem. If you tell them you'll reward the first person to come up with a solution, they will probably act selfishly in the strict sense of this word. This is a competition, not teamwork. You are not motivating the experts to help one another. At the very least, they will restrain from communicating knowledge and ideas that may help the competitors.

The best chance to see the problem solved is to offer equal rewards to everyone in the selected group. The experts will try again to get the personal benefit. However, the risk of not solving the problem and missing on the personal reward will motivate them to collaborate. They will be helping one another as much as possible. In this scenario, the selfishness underpins the teamwork.

In general, the need to minimize risk motivates communication of knowledge and sharing of ideas.

We are focusing here on teamwork to deal with uncertainty. Teamwork in the absence of identified risk is different. For example, if a group is building a house, the electrician doesn't need to share his knowledge of electrical installations with the plumber and the carpenter. Communication between them is still helpful and even necessary, but only for the purpose of implementing the house design *without surprises*. As their manager, you will pay them according to the required work, and you will not promote communication of new ideas. As humans, they all understand that the house will be more than the sum of electrical wires, pipes, walls, and cupboards. They may even feel a great pride knowing that their work with wires, pipes, and boards will end up as someone's home. However, they are not taking risks and they are happy with payments according to their measurable contributions.

Either way, all individuals need other people for their own survival and prosperity. Selfishness in the sense of a concern about personal benefit is not an obstacle but the driving force for teamwork. An obstacle is the tendency to rely on flawed cost–benefit analyses in the face of uncertainty. Too frequently, people feel they are giving more to the team and getting less in return, only to get nothing when the team falls apart. Another obstacle is the belief that controlling others is the way of securing a better personal benefit.

The man who gained world prominence from a holistic group he couldn't control.

Back in 1980, the world was at the peak of the Cold War between the Soviet-controlled Eastern Bloc and the

US-controlled Western Bloc. However, an unusually peaceful "meeting" between presidents and prime ministers from both sides of the Iron Curtain occurred on May 8, 1980. They rubbed shoulders with four kings and other officials from 128 different countries to honor the life and contribution to the world affairs by Josip Broz Tito—the life-president of former Yugoslavia—who had died four days earlier. At the time, this was the largest state funeral in history. The most notable absentee was Jimmy Carter, the serving US President, who sent his mother and the Vice President Walter Mondale to represent the United States.

Tito controlled his country of roughly twenty million people during his life, but he controlled no one else. So, why did all these heads of states and leaders travel to attend his funeral, exposing themselves to awkward meetings with some of their sworn enemies?

Tito's leadership in Yugoslavia dated back to 1939 when Joseph Stalin, the President of the Soviet Union, helped him take the role of General Secretary and lead the underground activities of the Communist Party of Yugoslavia. From this position, he marshalled guerilla troops to fight against Nazi's occupation. This was the only organized force on the territory of the defunct Yugoslav state. In 1943, the Western Allies recognized him as the leader of the Yugoslav resistance, which enabled him to redesign and control post-war Yugoslavia.

Tito had a close association with the communism in the Eastern Bloc, until he broke the relationship with Stalin in 1948. Following this event, the West helped Yugoslavia with financial and military aid, which evolved into an informal association with the Western Bloc in 1953. However, Tito resisted the idea of continued Westward course. He even jailed his possible successor, who was in favor of more democratic decision-making and was arguing against the model of one-party state. Instead, Tito reconciled his relationship with the post-Stalin leadership. During a conciliatory state visit in 1955, Stalin's successor signed a declaration that committed Soviet leaders to equality in relations with Yugoslavia.

Having positioned the country between the Eastern and the Western blocs, Tito engaged with like-minded heads of states outside the two blocs. To him, it didn't matter whether these people were dictators or democratically elected leaders. Together with the President of Egypt and the Prime Minister of India, he started promoting the concept of "active nonalignment," as an alternative not only to bloc politics but also to mere neutrality. Joined by the leaders of Egypt, India, Ghana, and Indonesia, Tito founded the Non-Aligned Movement and organized its first conference in Belgrade, the capital of Yugoslavia, in 1961.

Over time, the countries of the Non-Aligned Movement represented about 55 percent of the world's population. This was the political power that subdued the hostility of disparate leaders and state delegations from around the world as they traveled to Belgrade for Tito's funeral.

It's tempting to think of the Non-Aligned Movement as a third bloc. However, the massive membership in this organization evolved because there was no top–down control. Unlike the United Nations, the Non-Aligned Movement had no formal constitution and all members had equal weight within the organization. The movement would reach its positions regarding world affairs during its triennial summits and by consensus. The basis of this organization was the following five principles of restraint:

- Mutual respect for each other's territorial integrity and sovereignty.
- Mutual non-aggression.
- Mutual non-interference in domestic affairs.
- Equality and mutual benefit.
- Peaceful co-existence.

As a key benefit of the membership to Non-Aligned Movement, the countries were helping one another. For example, Yugoslavia provided military aid and arms supply to many developing countries, including states gaining independence from their colonial powers. In return, Yugoslav citizens enjoyed employment and healthy incomes from various projects in African and Middle East countries, as well as from sales of goods to oil-rich members of the organization.

Following the devastation from World War II, the life of Yugoslav citizens rapidly improved. Most citizens peacefully accepted the rapid shift from the pre-war kingdom to a post-war communism. Tito organized the federal and state governments in Yugoslavia by a progressive selection of suitable people from top to bottom, which was starkly different from the lack of hierarchical governing structure in the Non-Aligned Movement. He dealt with dissenting voices by punishment and removal from government positions. He was a dictator, but he was genuinely loved by the majority of ordinary citizens. They didn't even mind seeing him living like a king. Tito didn't pretend that his life was all about a humble service to the ordinary people. He didn't subscribe to this common hypocrisy by politicians at all levels and in all countries. He enjoyed his life like a monarch, with many palaces served by more than thousand people, a personal island, three zoos, special "blue train" with "imperial wagons," tens of boats, yachts, airplanes, and a bigger and more luxurious fleet of vehicles than the German Chancellor, French President, and the royal court of the UK together.[92] The pedantic bookkeeping of his administration shows that he was one of the most expensive rulers of the twentieth century. On the other hand, the ordinary citizens enjoyed what *The New York Times*'s obituary described as "a brand of Communism with free market forces, consumerism, Western publications at the newsstands, including nude centerfold magazines, a decision-sharing role for employees called workers' self-management, and, importantly, freedom for virtually all citizens to travel abroad and to return at will."[93] The obituary summarized the relationship between Tito's lavish lifestyle and his brand of communism by the following sentence: "In many ways, Tito seemed to typify the general Yugoslav approach to life—make it a pleasurable experience but do not compromise on honor or principle."[94]

It's fair to say that the Yugoslav president wanted as good life as possible for both himself and the citizens who were not disturbing the order he was trying to establish in the country. However, his top-down design of that order was a big problem. It worked fairly well while he was in power and able to impose a strict control, but his designed order collapsed spectacularly when the country disintegrated a decade or so after his death. As is usually the case, the social unrest was a response to a rapid economic downturn. His model of workers' self-management did not work. An even bigger problem was the utterly inefficient industry, which the government protected from external competition by a strict control of imported goods. The aim was to guard the fragile enterprises so that they could grow from the ashes of World War II. However, the control was far too strict and it went for too long.

So, Tito's control of his country ended up tragically for its citizens. In contrast, he didn't control the Non-Aligned Movement, which enabled its holistic emergence as an influential organization with Tito's image as one of the most powerful political leaders.

Top-down instructions don't make holistic teams.

Hierarchical structures and strict control work in armies fighting in a war. However, even in that case, the soldiers who risk their lives don't do it for the country without any consideration for their own benefit. Undoubtedly, their choices are limited, but they still try to get as much as possible in the circumstances. When fighting, soldiers don't want to sacrifice their lives for the country, but to defeat the enemy and to enjoy the rewards of their win.

An extreme case of limited choices for soldiers occurred toward the end of World War II when Japanese commanders decided to ask their pilots to kill themselves in attacks to Allied ships. These were the thousands of kamikaze pilots whose task was to destroy Allied ships by flying their aircraft into them. The commanders told selected pilots that they would be helping their country. The selected pilots "volunteered," but they had no choice. The account of a surviving kamikaze, Takehiko Ena, tells us that the kamikazes were not sacrificing their lives for the Emperor or the Empire. Takehiko survived because his plane crashed into the sea shortly after takeoff, so he couldn't complete the deadly mission. Surviving the crash, he lived to see the end of the deadly program when the war ended. When asked about kamikazes' motive, Takehiko said this: "On the surface, we were doing it for our country," and then he provided us with an insight below the surface by the following statement: "I just wanted to protect the father and mother I loved."[95]

This takes us to the central point about the concerns of individuals in a hierarchically organized group. Takehiko's immediate concern was his own life. This may seem selfish from the Emperor's perspective but, from Takehiko's perspective, he could not continue helping others once he died. To take care of yourself first is not a selfish attitude. The safety instructions in commercial airplanes advise passengers that, in the event of loss of cabin pressure, they should secure their own oxygen masks first and then help children and others who may need help. This makes perfect sense; a parent trying to help a child first could lose consciousness in the absence of oxygen, which would be a tragic altruism for both of them.

Going back to Takehiko's example, it shows that the next

level of concern was not for the Emperor and the country but for his mother and father. Putting love aside, the mindset that his deadly mission was going to protect his mother and father rather than the country is rational.

In general, the people who we can help the most are our partners and immediate family. The next group of people in terms of our ability to help are our co-workers.

Many of us work in groups that report to a manager and, in larger organizations, the management structure continues through medium- and senior-level managers, all the way to the CEO or the president. This type of hierarchical structure is common for both military and civil organizations. On paper, it creates order because all individuals act in response to instructions from the top. It is an elegant and simple organizational model, assuming a kind of mechanistic world and actions that resemble programmed robots. In reality, the world is uncertain, and people don't act like robots; instead, they make free-will decisions to deal with uncertainty.

We are not saying that the top–down instructions by the management don't matter. They do and they are crucial for the success or failure of an organization. When these instructions make sense to their recipients, they respond adequately and everything works like a machine. So, if you are a manager, the best option you have is to explain the purpose and the benefit of your instructions. If you are unable to convince your inferiors for some reason, the next best scenario is for them to trust you. Beyond that, you could exercise the power you have as a manager to make military-type orders. The Japanese Emperor during World War II had the power to implement the plan of pilot suicides in his attempt to defend the country. The CEO and the high-level managers in a company have the power to sack workers.

When executives exercise this kind of power, they claim their actions are in the interest of the group they represent.

The Japanese Emperor wanted the kamikaze to believe that he acted with responsibility to protect the people of Japan. An inherent assumption here is that, if the Emperor surrendered, the people he was responsible for would suffer. With this assumption, the Emperor's selfishness was the necessary trait for his ability to help others; it meant that what was good for him was good for the inferiors.

Analogously to the Emperor's power to kill pilots, managers in companies can fire people. In some instances, this is necessary to create a healthier working environment. However, exercising this power is not nearly sufficient to create a strong organization. In fact, imposing power by top-down orders doesn't build thriving groups. Google's executive chairman and former CEO, Eric Schmidt, did have a point when he said that "managers serve the team."[96]

Yet, the reality is that managers also have to serve shareholders' interests.[97]

As a manager, you have to serve both shareholders' interests and your team but—let's be honest—you wouldn't do it without some personal interest. What makes a group strong is not a kind of pure altruistic service but aligned interests of its individuals. This means that, as a manager, it doesn't help to hide your own interests and to pretend that you are simply serving others. Nobody will believe it. People despise hypocrisy. If the people in your team have to guess your interests, you cannot control their cynicism. On the other hand, if they see that your interests are aligned with theirs, they will trust you and will serve you in return, for everyone is doing it for his or her own benefit. That way, you will receive much more than lean responses to your requests, because the team members will feel safe to ask questions and will be motivated to communicate ideas. The result will be achievements beyond the limits of your plan. The team will be more than the sum of its members.

Think beyond hierarchical charts to see that people are in the center of their own circles.

Different from service-up and service-down relationships, a typical hierarchical chart assumes top–down instructions and bottom–up responses. It shows a CEO on the top, senior managers at the level below, and further down middle-level managers and team leaders. This kind of chart defines no more than your power position in your organization. However, this chart doesn't define you as a person and doesn't determine your overall life experience.

It's better to think of your own organizational chart, where you are right in the center with a link to your work place, but also with radial links to your family, friends, doctors, advisors, and all others who you need in your life. If you are a manager, you should recognize that your power is limited to rewards and penalties, meaning that you are not the owner of your inferiors because they are all in the center of their own organizational charts.

You may wonder now what trick is behind the sweet organizational model placing us all in the center of our own circles, so that we can all focus on our self-interests. Wouldn't conflicting self-interests inhibit teamwork?

These conflicts appear as unresolvable when we think in the zero-sum framework of cost–benefit equations, where the cost is what we give and the benefit is what we take. A typical conflict scenario is the interest of employers to cut cost against the interest of employees to earn more. A classic example is Henry Ford's situation in the early 1900s, as he was transitioning to mass production of his best-selling Model T automobile.

Before settling on the design of Model T in 1908, the majority of the workforce in Ford's factory were highly skilled mechanics and managers. These workers exercised "broad discretion in the direction of their own work and that of their helpers,"[98] so we can assume that they felt a degree of pride and self-importance. In our terminology, they could consider themselves in the center of their own worlds.

The introduction of mass production with Model T changed the character of Ford's workforce. The work became more menial, consisting of finely divided and clearly specified tasks. Learning these tasks was fast and easy, so the workers earned their wages by performing routine tasks rapidly. One of the laborers described his work as repeatedly "putting on Nut No. 86." Another worker stressed that you had to keep repeating a routine task from the time "you become a number in the morning until the bell rings for quitting time." Feeling as mere numbers, they lost their pride and self-importance. They could no longer feel like in the center of their own worlds.

Ford's laborers were not happy with the working conditions, but the mass-production approach was yielding the projected financial results. The price of Model T dropped from more than $800 to less than $300, and the company profit rose from just over $4 million in 1910 to $20 million in 1914. This was achieved with the minimum wage of $2.34 a day, in line with how much other companies were paying their workers.

On January 5, 1914, Ford announced what they called "the greatest revolution in the matter of rewards for its workers ever known to the industrial world."[99] The cornerstone of this revolution was a decision to increase the minimum pay from $2.34 to $5.00 a day and to shorten the working day from nine to eight hours. The wage increase meant an increase in the company's costs in 1914 by about $10 million—a half of the projected annual profit. This was a shocking decision to increase company's costs for the benefit of laborers.

Some analyses of this remarkable event suggest that Ford was trying to solve a problem due to a large turnover of workers. In 1913, the company had to hire more than 50,000 men in order to maintain the average labor force of less than

14,000. This was a significantly higher turnover in comparison to other companies at the time, but the cost of replacing all these people was insignificant.[100] The training costs for the low-skilled labor were negligible and a lot of people were looking for work.

However, Ford did not rely on these cost calculations, judging by the following statement: "We wanted to pay these wages so that the business would be on a lasting foundation. We were building for the future. A low wage business is always insecure."[101] Ford sensed that the business was insecure because he saw that the productivity of 14,000 laborers *on average* could be different from the productivity of stable workforce of 14,000. Instead of relying on calculations based on average workforce, his management focused on the behavior of individual workers.

An example of this focus is when the company's personnel manager investigated an abrupt fall in the output of a drop-hammer operator. They found that the operator's wife was very ill and his mind was preoccupied by fear about her health and the incurred medical expenses. In essence, they discovered that the operator could not leave his personal worries and interests at home to perform like a machine when he was at work. The automobiles the company was making were all alike—one automobile was like another automobile—but this was not the case with its workers, even though this was an inherent assumption in the cost and profit calculations.

When the management learned about the operator's debt for medical expenses, they paid it off and his productivity jumped up. To an eye looking beyond the usual cost and profit calculations, this would indicate a direct link between a better-paid workforce and productivity. So, it's likely that Ford's management was trying to improve productivity. They realized that good productivity doesn't come from a worker who feels like a number from "the morning until the bell rings for quitting time." In our words, they realized that good productivity comes from a worker with his own identity, feeling in the center of his own circle of interests. This would be the reason for their decision to award the pay increase from $2.34 to $5.00 as profit sharing rather than as wages, and only to workers who wouldn't debauch the additional money. To carry out this provision, the company set a Sociological Department with a team of 150 inspectors. (It's the kind of moral policing that would not work in today's world.) The aim was to reward workers who were living in clean surroundings, taking baths, and saving to buy one's own house; on the other hand, "excessive drinking, gambling, untidiness, consumption of unwholesome foods, and lack of enthusiasm for putting money regularly into a savings account were all potential grounds for exclusion from the profit."[102]

Ford's "revolution in the matter of rewards for its workers" succeeded. The employees were happy with the pay raise and with the company's concern about their sense of dignity. It's telling that some workers proudly wore their company badges to dances and other social events.[103] Most laborers received twice as much money as the typical wage at the time, and the company increased its profit from the predicted $20 million in 1914 to over $30 million in that year and over $40 million in 1915.

This is an example of a holistic change—creating more for everyone in the organization. If the company didn't introduce this change, the declining morale of its workers would've reduced the profit, if not wiping it out completely. Ford's management sensed that the newly introduced mass-production method created uncertainty, and this example shows that the uncertainty presented both danger and opportunity for the company. The example also shows that the zero-sum assumption in the cost-versus-profit calculations is misleading because it ignores this uncertainty.

Make sure your self-interest is enlightened.

There was no certainty Ford's pay-raise revolution would end up with positive results. Because of this uncertainty, some analysts suggested a different motive for his decision—"a desire to be magnanimous," or what they also called "an altruistic impulse."[104] It could be argued that Ford didn't serve the interest of the shareholders when he exercised his control to implement the pay-raise idea (at the time, he owned 58.5 percent of the company). He risked shareholders' profits for workers' pay-raise. Yet giving such a large profit away was not an act of a pure altruistic impulse. The management could neither prevent the workers from leaving nor force them to deliver the expected outputs, which Ford saw as a risk for the long-term foundation of the business. He decided to act by risking the forecasted profit. In contrast to this risk, the act of "a wealthy industrialist sharing profits with workers on such a scale"[105] was certain to generate glowing newspaper headlines and editorials around the world. Seeing this act as a desire for publicity, while attempting to solve a problem, we have an example of what philosophers, politicians, and businesspeople call "enlightened self-interest."

Among numerous descriptions of enlightened self-interest, the following sentences encapsulate the key elements of this important concept: "While most of our actions are motivated by a desire to fulfill inner needs and personal desires, acts of enlightened self-interest serve the well-being of others as well. Enlightened self-interest means that everybody wins."[106] Essentially, this concept is the link between our desire to fulfill inner needs and the holistic effect when everybody wins.

Actually, aligning self-interest with the common interest of a group is not just about winning. It's also about not losing; in other words, it's about creating an environment for fast and effective resolution of problems caused by uncertain events. A good example is Toyota's manufacturing system, which evolved into what is now called the lean manufacturing philosophy. Toyota's strict control and tenacious execution of all manufacturing tasks by its workers reduced, but did not eradicate, uncertainty. To minimize the risk from uncertain events, the original Toyota system empowered the workers to stop the production line when someone observed an unexpected deviation. With a focus on individual productivity, the workers would be motivated to pass on small deviations, which could subsequently degrade quality or even develop into a big problem. However, Toyota's management motivated the line operators to halt the production process by turning on a light hanging from the factory ceiling. Inviting others to take a look, this enabled the most informed decision regarding the observed deviation.

The lean thinking goes further by developing employees' autonomy in problem solving rather than telling them what to do. The purpose is not to modify formulas and implement new processes, but rather to ensure continuous improvement and adaptation to changing conditions. In this approach, all individuals are in the business of quality assurance and adding value, as distinct from merely performing prescribed work. This is a clear break from the principles of scientific management, formulated by Frederick Winslow Taylor—an American mechanical engineer who championed ideas for improved industrial efficiency. In 1911, Taylor summarized his teaching in his book *The Principles of Scientific Management*.[107] In a nutshell, these principles are about finding and implementing "one right way" of doing something.

Taylorism has a scientific appeal, but it can easily morph into a counterproductive top–down implementation of the one-right-way philosophy. A good example is the decision of Boeing's senior management to launch their 737 Max model as the one-right-way to respond to Airbus's competition with fuel-efficient engines. All feedback to the management about safety concerns fell on deaf ears, in a sharp contrast to the system of empowering workers to halt production. The observed aerodynamic instability of the aircraft was not a showstopper for the senior management. For them, this was a problem to solve, far from a bottom–up dictate of what should or shouldn't be the right way. Accordingly, they ordered the infamous development of software as a fix to the mechanical instability. The result was two fatal crashes, grounded fleet of 737 Max airplanes, huge financial losses, and tarnished image of a flagship company. This is a modern example of what is sometimes called *Vasa* syndrome.

Vasa was a magnificent warship, built in the early seventeenth century to scare the enemies of the Swedish king. It was an expensive warship, costing over 5 percent of Sweden's gross national product. The Swedish navy launched it on August 10, 1628, but it sank in Stockholm harbor after sailing less than a mile. This impactful failure became a case study for business experts.

The construction of Vasa began at the time when the Swedish navy was fighting Denmark, Russia, and Poland. The king discovered that Denmark was planning to build a ship with two gun-decks and more cannons than in his single-deck fleet. He immediately ordered the addition of a second deck, changing the 32 guns in the original Vasa design to 64 bronze cannons. The builders executed the order and Admiral Klas Fleming tested its stability in the summer of 1628. The test consisted of thirty men running from one side to the other. After the third run, they halted the test because the ship was tilting dangerously under the weight of only thirty people. Nonetheless, Fleming did not postpone the commissioning of the ship, commenting that "the shipbuilder has built ships before and he should not be worried."[108] However, the ship sank as soon as it departed for its maiden voyage.

According to existing information, Fleming was a coward

and willing to remain silent for the sake of his own career advancement and job security.[109] Focused on himself, he didn't think about the impact of his decision on others. His idea that a shipbuilder knows how to build ships was an overgeneralization to justify his negligence. The effects of such a shortsighted selfishness are destructive, in contrast to the team-building effects of enlightened selfishness.

Fleming's job was to test and commission the ship. However, he acted as if his job was to tell what the king wanted to hear.

Speaking in general, telling your superiors falsehoods they want to hear could end up being either enlightened or destructive selfishness. If telling fibs would avoid an unnecessary conflict, then it's helpful to do it. Keeping the focus on the real task by avoiding unnecessary arguments helps the group's performance. On the other hand, it's a destructive selfishness to agree with your superiors and mislead them in pursuit of your personal benefit at the expense of the group.

The situation is slippery when people fear punishment from the top and see no better option but to tell their superiors falsehoods they want to hear. This situation indicates an overzealous application of Taylor's principles of scientific management. It happens when the management firmly believes in their one right way, and the people underneath have to implement the orders to the letter. Then, punishment becomes the method of preventing any aberrations from the right way. If the people implementing the orders see problems, their fear of punishment prevents them from providing the needed bottom–up feedback. The situation is even worse if they have to deliver false positive feedback, exacerbating the problem and accelerating the breakdown of this system.

Fear is a powerful emotion. It evolved to protect us from an imminent danger. However, its long-term impact on interpersonal relationships in a group is complex. Other emotions also affect these relationships, and it's not as simple as saying anger is bad whereas happiness is good for the team. Let's see why this is so.

9

Build Teams on the Platform of Emotions

Sometimes, our emotions cause problems. However, suppressing our emotions will not solve those problems and turn us into purely rational humans. It's wrong to think that powerful emotions are our enemy—quite the opposite. The neural system at the root of these emotions enabled our predecessors to survive and evolve. We inherited this primary neural system and we still need it.

Think of a driver who slams the brakes as a pedestrian suddenly decides to cross the road. This is the primary neural system in action:

1. The driver's eyes sense the unexpected event and create neural signals.

2. The signals travel through neurons linked by synapses that are established during driver's training.

3. The neural signals fire muscle cells in the leg, which is the needed action in response to the unexpected event.

This primary *sensing–processing–actuation* chain is fundamental and is necessary for quick subconscious actions. Only after the car stops, the driver in our example becomes aware that a pedestrian could've been killed. This awareness emerges from massive neuron firing and stampeding signals through the most complex neural networks of the brain. The driver feels this neural activity as bursting emotions, accompanied by physical effects such as accelerated heart beats and sweating hands.

The driver needs to calm down after avoiding the fatal accident, but this doesn't help anticipate the danger. Trying to control emotions consciously is helpful, but a quick and adequate subconscious response to a surprising event is even better. Hence, we should focus on the knowledge memorized in our synapses, because this knowledge will guide the neural signals for our subconscious actions in the future.

We inherit some of that synaptic knowledge; an example is fear of snakes. When an animal sees a snake, the subconscious muscle actions also include the facial expression of fear. That way, the animal alerts others in the group about the danger. Charles Darwin's book, *The Expression of the Emotions in Man and Animals*[110], points to a high similarity and a link between emotional expressions in animals and humans. At least six basic emotions relate to facial expressions that are universal to all humans, regardless of culture and educational background—fear, anger, disgust, sadness, happiness, and surprise.

Link the facial expressions of emotions to the knowledge they communicate.

The facial expressions we are talking about here are subconscious responses to unexpected events. Assume you are in a meeting with your team leader to convey unexpected information. Even before you hear any words in response, you can know a lot from the facial expression of the developing emotion.

Assume the information you are providing is about a patent from another company, protecting the intellectual property your team needs for your biggest project. *Fear* on the leader's face would communicate knowledge of danger. For example, the leader may know that the patent assignee is a dangerous competitor. Even if you hear from him no more than, "Leave it with me, and I'll think about it," you should know that he is poised to run away from the protected property.

Anger displays preparedness to fight, which is the opposite of running away. Let's turn the patent scenario around, so that you tell the leader about an infringement of your protected intellectual property by another company. The facial expression of anger would reveal his knowledge that a legal action could defeat the infringing company.

However, the information about the infringing company may result in the facial expression of *sadness*. We could translate this expression into the following words: The leader knows how unfavorable this scenario is, but also knows that very little can be done against that specific company.

Let's say now that you are presenting to the leader a plan how to get some reward for the group—or, alternatively, how to get out of a trouble—but the plan boils down to disguised cheating. Seeing the facial expression of *disgust*, you should immediately know that she has no intention whatsoever to get

involved. She is neither angry nor fearful, so she is neither fighting nor running away; the message is that your thinking has no place in her team.

Like all of us, you like to see *happiness*. Assume you are passing a new information to your leader, but you don't know the actual value of what you are saying. Happiness on her face would tell you that she knows the information is favorable.

Finally, it may happen that your unexpected information elicits *surprise*. Apart from not expecting to hear what you are saying, this would also tell you that the leader doesn't know whether the new information is favorable or not. This could change as he gets the

time to think about it, but the facial expression of surprise reveals the initial lack of knowledge.

Don't fear imaginary failure.

People experience a wide spectrum of fear intensities—from terror to trepidation—but the common feature is that some danger causes this emotion. If the danger is real, then the fear works in our favor as it guides us into safety. However, our uncertain world tricks too many of us to imagine dangers. For example, fear of *failure* is common, but instead of saving us, it frequently results in failure to succeed. As Maryann wrote in her book, *Lessons from the Edge*, "A desire to succeed can strengthen you, but a *fear of failure can immobilize you*."[III] A problem with the fear of failure is lost opportunities.

Too many researchers lost their opportunity to develop blue light-emitting diodes (LEDs), even as they knew that blue LEDs would revolutionize office, home, and street lighting. Of course, these applications use *white* light in shades such as cool and warm, but a source of the high-energy blue photons is needed to create the spectrum of white light.

The material in all white LED lighting today is gallium nitride. Researchers observed emission of blue light from gallium nitride in 1950s and then again in 1972.[112] However, it took another twenty-two years to see commercial blue LEDs in 1994.[113] The key problem was researchers' trepidation that prevented them from trying this material. The feature they feared was a high density of misplaced atoms in the crystalline structure. These defects in the crystalline order didn't pose any direct danger. They are only visible by special microscopes but are not harmful nanoparticles. What the researchers feared was the reactions of their colleagues if they decided to try this material and failed. In 1980s, the focus was on a nice-looking material—zinc selenide—with a million times lower density of spatially disordered atoms. Not only was the nice-looking material more popular, but gallium nitride was also actively discouraged by statements that it had no future.

Universities encourage their researchers to try and find new things. In addition to teaching, this is the core business at universities. In this business, the researchers routinely turn around failed trials into new knowledge, whether this would be a new theory or a new direction for additional experiments. However, it was difficult to sell in this way failed experiments with gallium nitride. People would say it was stupid to spend time and money playing with such a defective material when there was a much cleaner option. The fear from being regarded as stupid by the research community flocked almost everyone into a worldwide group working with zinc selenide. Almost endless failed experiments and theories didn't really matter. The researchers were happily exchanging their experiences and new theories in published papers and at conferences. There was no trepidation to continue this work because there was no danger to be seen by the peers as a stupid person.

At the 1992 conference of the Japan Society of Applied Physics, approximately 500 researchers attended the sessions on zinc selenide. In contrast, the gallium-nitride session attracted five people. Three of them would eventually win and share the Nobel Prize for the invention and commercialization of blue LED. These three people were Professor Isamu Akasaki as the Session Chair, his student Hiroshi Amano as the speaker, and Mr. Shuji Nakamura in the audience.

In his Nobel Lecture[114], Nakamura told us his reason for the decision to work on gallium nitride for blue LEDs. The reason was not his confidence that a successful development of this LED was possible. His objective was to get a PhD degree. In the late 1980s, Nakamura worked at the University of Florida as a visiting researcher. Because he didn't have a PhD and had no published scientific papers, his colleagues there treated him as a technician. This relegated his role to helping others, without an opportunity for his name to appear on published papers and patents. Frustrated, he looked for the easiest way to solve this problem. At the time, he could be awarded a PhD degree in Japan without the need to enroll in a university. All he needed to do was publish five scientific papers. He was confident he could do it if he avoided the fierce competition by joining the niche work by Akasaki and Amano.

A US-based conference in 1993 showed that only three notable researchers were working on gallium nitride: Akasaki, Amano, and Nakamura. Thousands of other people were in the group devoted to the nice-looking zing selenide. Nakamura was not in the big ruling group by his own choice, and he didn't fear their derisive opinion. It was not his aim to develop blue LED and he didn't care about the prevailing view that gallium nitride had no future. His aim was to publish at least five papers and, with that aim, he felt safe working alongside Akasaki and Amano. At the time he was employed by Nichia Chemical Corporation in Japan, and he extorted funding for the development of blue LED by threats to resign from the company.[115] These resignation threats were extraordinarily risky in terms of future employment in Japan, so they demonstrate his commitment to the aim of obtaining a PhD degree and his confidence in the paper-publishing plan.

Nakamura's success ended up being much bigger than his plan. Not only did he receive a PhD in 1994, but Nichia also manufactured commercial blue LEDs in the same year. The road toward twenty-first century lighting with LEDs was open.

The density of gallium-nitride defects, feared by the scientists in 1980s, remains high in today's LED material. It is much higher than the perceived threshold for efficient light emission, and not even close to the levels of the nice-looking zinc selenide. Fear from the imagined certainty that these were killer defects prevented highly-qualified researchers from trying gallium nitride, even when the potential reward was as great as a revolution in lighting—a great benefit for both the society and the innovators.

A way of unleashing anger to achieve a positive outcome.

Signaling preparedness to fight, anger is a confrontational emotion, and it can damage a relationship permanently. Allowing yourself to feel anger also makes you a less effective thinker. Your cognitive brain loses its edge as your limbic system—parts of the brain that deal with emotions and memory—becomes more dominant. However, the *appearance* of anger, rather than the actual experience of it, can be part of a last-ditch attempt to resolve a stubborn issue. The following example illustrates how this could happen.

Pat was a team leader in a large organization. Her team was racking up excellent results with a great promise to diversify the core business of the company. This created the need to strengthen the core activities, and the senior management decided to merge the team into a larger group with Bob as a newly appointed manager.

According to the set structure, Bob was reporting to the senior management on behalf of the whole group. He didn't consult with Pat about reports related to her team, but she received copies of some of his e-mails to various upper-level managers. Pat didn't like how Bob was presenting the activities and performance of the key people in her team, so she sent follow-up emails to explain that they worked with her in a different direction.

After a while, Bob involved the Human Resource Management in discussions about the performance of Pat's team. She sensed that Bob could be preparing the ground for an unsatisfactory performance assessment of the people in her team. Worried about this possibility, Pat asked him to explain his intentions. At the beginning of their meeting, he started talking about a mismatch between his key performance indicators and the work of Pat's team. She tried to explain the merit of the work her people were doing in terms of the great potential benefits for the group and for the whole company. She also mentioned the support by the senior management. They were running in circles. Frustrated, Pat deliberately raised her voice. When he countered her, she talked over him, stressing that her intention was to defend her people against any attempt to remove them from their positions. With her angry voice, Pat drew a line in the sand and essentially dared Bob to cross it.

The following day, Bob filed a formal complaint against Pat. The rationale was her "yelling" in the meeting room. The first response by the senior management was to offer Pat professional anger-management support. She refused it, explaining that this would be like taking an aspirin without any attempt to find the cause of the temperature. She added that Bob's dismissive attitude regarding her concern was simply anger expressed differently. Asked how she would resolve the conflict, she insisted the best way would be to find the root cause of the conflict. Senior management decided to send Pat and Bob to a professional mediator.

The mediator's view was that a miscommunication rather than an ulterior motive was usually the root cause of this kind of conflict. He asked Pat and Bob to explain to one another their actions and intentions. Bob confirmed that he understood Pat's situation and her intentions. However, regarding some of his actions, he stated that he couldn't provide an explanation at that point of time. The moderator asked him how much time he would need to offer his explanation. While Bob was quiet, thinking about the situation he found himself in, Pat made an offer. She said she was prepared to move past the conflict and to help with Bob's management tasks as much as possible, but in return Bob had to (1) offer a formal apology and (2) promise not to interfere with the work of her team if he wasn't able to help them.

Bob determined he had nothing to lose by accepting the offer. The senior management was pleased with that outcome, and even more so with the aggregate results that Bob's group achieved after the initial conflict with Pat.

Using disgust to express moral outrage.

Maryann worked for a trade association of high technology companies for seven years, and in fact, one of the reasons why this author partnership works well is that she worked closely with several electronics engineers. She rose through the ranks to become head of her department, a position that required quarterly presentations to the board of directors. Having shared the contents of one of her presentations with a senior colleague, she was shocked, dismayed, and visibly disgusted when he wove in a criticism of one of her proposals before she'd even had a chance to present it.

She felt the offense was so grave that she allowed the look of disgust to remain on her face, even when she rose to give her presentation. Then, in a straightforward way, she noted that one of the proposals she was about to make had already been criticized, but she invited the board to consider it anyway.

Several of the board members later expressed privately to Maryann that her disgust was justified. One of them represented a technology giant that quickly offered her an enviable position, which she accepted.

Hiding her disgust would have protected the colleague and still allowed her to proceed in a forceful and dignified way. Showing her disgust, however, drew attention to the colleague's deceit—a trait that board members did not want in a corporate officer and had a right to know about.

The value of disconnecting sadness from causality.

This is a true story with the name changed to protect the privacy of the individual. Tom was an accountant, engaged to be married. His young practice was thriving, and his personal life, filled with happiness and anticipation. Walking side-by-side with his fiancée on a downtown street, a truck jumped the curb and killed her.

For Tom-the-accountant, it was essential that the numbers added up and the books balanced. But when Tom-the-grieving-fiancé applied that same order- and causality-driven approach to his personal life, it nearly ruined his professional one. He was obsessed with trying to make sense of a random act that involved a truck driver having a heart attack at the exact moment he and his girlfriend happened to be on the sidewalk that day. It drove him to such distraction that, at work, he would look at the numbers on a page and question every calculation he made, every conclusion he drew.

At the recommendation of a friend, Tom engaged with a therapist certified in Emotionally Focused Therapy (EFT). He was introduced to the concept of a "felt sense" of events. Instead of trying to make sense of tragedy and deny its randomness—fruitless cognitive exercises—he learned to shift into a deep appreciation for what his emotions could tell him about how to heal. The therapeutic work he did not only helped him grieve in a healthy way and move forward with his personal life, but also return fully to the career he enjoyed.

Trevor Crow Mullineaux, Maryann's co-author of *Forging Healthy Connections*, is an EFT therapist, who summarizes the experience like this: "If a physician asked you, 'Where does it hurt?' or 'Where does it itch?' you could probably give an answer without hesitating. In putting the concept of 'felt sense' to work in your life, you make the same kind of link between emotion and your body—and you give yourself and people around you, a powerful tool to support health and healing."[116] Going back to the title of the chapter, you are building on a platform of emotions to heal and move forward. Thinking through the "why" of the accident would not position Tom to accomplish that.

Make sure you understand the relationship between happiness and money.

David Geffen, an American music and movie magnate, once made the following statement about the relationship between happiness and money: "Anybody who thinks money will make you happy, hasn't got money."[117] On the other hand, most people relate better to the following remark by Mark Twain: "The lack of money is the root of all evil."[118,119] These two maxims are not contradicting one another, as it may seem at first glance. Twain's quote is about the lack of money for necessities, whereas Geffen's saying is about money above a necessity threshold.

Two psychologists, Daniel Kahneman and Angus Deaton, put a number on the necessity threshold in a paper they published in August 2010.[120] The result came from the authors' study at the Center for Health and Well-being at Princeton University. In the study, they distinguished the concept of *experienced happiness* from the concept of *life satisfaction*. The measure of experienced happiness was the frequency and intensity of happy events, reduced by the frequency and intensity of unhappy events (events giving rise to sadness, anger, anxiety, stress, worry, and so on). On the other hand, the definition of life satisfaction was person's thoughts about his or her life, hence unrelated to actual events.

The key result of the study was this: Life satisfaction raises steadily with a higher income, whereas the experienced happiness increases only up to the annual income of about $75,000 and there is no further progress with the income growth above this threshold.

Discussing the results, the authors of the study made the following observation: "In the context of income, a $100 raise does not have the same significance for a financial services executive as for an individual earning the minimum wage, but a doubling of their respective incomes might have a similar impact on both."[121] This appears as a simple concept, but let's unpack it.

Assume a person earning the minimum wage wins $1,000. This significant change is a happy event, associated with intense neuron firing as the person works out how best to utilize the win. If this person subsequently reaches the annual income of $100,000 and wins $1,000 again, this would no longer be a significant change. The steady increase from $100,000 to $101,000 would barely register in the thinking neurons and would no longer be experienced as a happy event.

An income leap would be a significant change, so a lot of people try it, and some manage to achieve it. However, this approach can trigger a long chain of unpredictable events. The story of Dan Price, the CEO of Seattle-based Gravity Payments, is an example.

Dan founded this credit-card-processing company with his brother, Lucas Price, in 2004. Initially, it was a 50–50 split, but in 2008 they changed it to two thirds for Dan and one third for Lucas, who would also receive $400,000 in cash and would remain on the two-man board of the company. In 2012, Dan jacked up his salary to $1 million—apparently several times higher than the salaries of executives in similar companies.[122] A year later, Dan asked for an increase to $1.4 million, but his brother resisted. In an unexpected response, Dan suggested that his salary should be $5.5 million, which was more than half of the company's revenue.[123] In terms of total income from 2010 to 2014, Dan made $6 million, whereas Lucas's income was around $150,000 a year. The scene seemed set for a dramatic chain of events.

On March 16, 2015, Lucas served his brother with a lawsuit, and filed it formally with the court on April 24, 2015. The allegation was that Dan Price "improperly used his majority control of the company to pay himself excessive compensation and to deprive Lucas of the benefits of ownership in Gravity Payments."[124] On April 13, between the dates when Lucas served and formally filed the lawsuit, Dan dropped a bombshell. He invited *The New York Times* and NBC News to cover a surprising announcement of his decision to raise the minimum salaries of all employees to $70,000. At the time, the average wage of the 120 employees at Gravity Payments was less than $50,000. He also announced that he was cutting his own salary from $1.1 million down to $70,000 to help cover the increased cost. According to Dan, the number of $70,000 was in line with the study by Kahneman and Deaton, and he wanted this salary to increase the experienced happiness of all his employees. According to the study, the happiness value of extra dollars would be marginal beyond this threshold.

Soon after the announcement, he received invitations to appear on *The Today Show* and also on *Good Morning America*. He flew to New York and did about 25 live TV interviews in three days. In August 2015, academics from the Harvard Business School used Dan's scheme as a case study.[125] In November 2015, *Inc.* magazine put him on its cover with a story titled "Is This the Best Boss in America?" Bernie Sanders, the prominent US senator from Vermont, appeared with Dan Price on MSNBC and tweeted, "At a time of massive wealth and income inequality in our country, Mr. Price set an example others should learn from."[126] However, some people detested his example of addressing income inequality. Two employees left his company, saying that the scheme was unfair to higher earners. Certain media outlets ridiculed him.

Writing about the worldwide interest in his move, Dan states that he received "praise, criticism, and outright scorn from journalists, pundits, businesspeople, and ordinary folks who were either inspired or horrified by the decision." According to him, people were trying to work out whether he was making a statement about income inequality, or he was "a militant socialists out to destroy capitalism," or a philanthropist, or maybe he was just "pulling a publicity stunt designed to drum up attention" for his small company.[127] However, as an echo from Henry Ford's famous pay raise, Dan offered the most succinct description of his motive to an *Esquire* journalist: "Hey, I'm a narcissist, like all millennials. Did I raise the salaries for purely benevolent reasons? Yes, but I also wanted to be a hero."[128]

In another similarity with Ford's act of enlightened selfishness, Dan's scheme worked for his employees and for the company. Five years after the announcement of the $70,000 minimum wage, Dan tweeted the positive effects: the business tripled, staff who own homes grew tenfold, 401(k) contributions grew tenfold, 70 percent of employees paid off debt, staff having kids soared tenfold, and turnover dropped in half with staff engaged at work being double the national average.[129]

For many, Dan Price was successful with his aim to be a hero, but a profound sadness ended up tainting the success.

According to his own words, Dan was loved by two people, his wife and his brother. But he needed more than the love and the money.

This need can get anybody in trouble, but we all share it. Our advanced brains are the reason we take what seems as unnecessary risks. *Unlike animals that can rest peacefully in the absence of hunger signals in their neurons, our brains are itchy for fun.* We need to fire our complex neurons, and the tricky question is how to do it.

Like many others, Dan tried the road of successive money leaps. Once he was on the salary of $1 million, the subsequent increase to $1.1 million was an insignificant change. As Kahneman and Deaton noted, something like doubling the income would've had a psychological impact. Dan tried that, but it backfired. He lost the love of his brother, even though he won the lawsuit in July 2015. His brother no longer speaks to him. He also lost the love of his wife. Their marriage ended in 2012—the year when his salary jumped up to $1 million. Six months after his $70,000 dollar announcement, she accused him of abuse.[130] Although his employees could see his money sharing with them as an enlightened selfishness, it seems his action looked differently from the perspective of his ex-wife.

A hero for some people, he became an obnoxious person for others.

Do not aim for a life without surprises.

We don't make wrong calls when we can predict the future impact of our decisions. That's why we focus on learning and building knowledge that can help us predict the future. The question then is whether this is the best road to happiness. For example, Daniel Gilbert argues in his book, *Stumbling on Happiness*, that "stumbling" of humans to build happiness is related to the limited ability to predict the future.[131]

To think about this question, let's start a "dream" in which we are somehow granted perfect knowledge, so that we are able to predict and avoid all unfavorable events in the future. In this dream, there is no longer uncertainty. There is neither need nor possibility to introduce *new* and better rules, to create *new* knowledge, or to design *new* products,

Car mechanics are able to follow perfect manufacturing processes, which eliminates all surprises with cars. Chefs teach their apprentices perfect cooking recipes, removing any meal variations. Meteorologists deliver weather predictions with certainty, putting an end to weather surprises. Powerful computers provide advanced predictions of sports games, so the scores are no longer uncertain. The complete knowledge wipes out unexpected twists in stories and movies. There are no longer jokes with punchlines that make us laugh when we get the joke after the initial surprise.

Everybody knows the future with certainty, but nobody is happy without the uncertainties of sports games, without the real stories and movies, and without the funny jokes. Many are dispirited without the chance to create *new* products and *new* knowledge. Some people feel miserable without the chance to double their income. There is no happiness in this paradigm of perfection.

Luckily, this suffocating certainty doesn't exist, and we can have fun. It may be disconcerting to let randomness taint the teaching that we should aspire for perfection, but it's also liberating to know that the world is imperfect. Seeing why the exclusive focus on certainty leads to disappointments, we should focus on our emotional intelligence to minimize these unpleasant surprises.

10

Utilize Brain Plasticity to Improve Your Emotional Intelligence

The prevalent contemporary teaching considers emotional intelligence as the "ability to monitor one's own and others' feelings and emotions, to discriminate among them and to use this information to guide one's thinking and actions."[132] So, instead of fast emotional actions, the idea is to think about the emotions first and then act.

A simple example of how this can work is when you receive an email urgently asking you to change the password for your bank account, and if you don't click on the offered link, thieves can steal your money. Instead of allowing fear to drive your action and to click on the offered link, you should calm down and consider the likely possibility this is a phishing scam. Give yourself time to inspect it, call the bank, and if it is a scam, delete it.

To take a more complex example, assume your supervisor surprises you with a question about your willingness to leave the current position and move to another department. In this situation, the following wisdom seems the most relevant: Don't make a decision if you feel sad; don't speak if you feel angry; and don't promise anything if you feel happy. Speaking in general, the idea is to control your emotions and, if possible, to sense what feeling is behind the supervisor's action. Clearly, this is a recipe for no immediate action. But could this work? Does it mean you should show no more than a stone face and say no more than something like, "Let me think about it"?

In reality, you are likely to ask questions, initiating a conversation that would reflect your mindset. If the meeting is face-to-face, the body language and the facial expressions are also likely to signal how you feel about the proposal. Assume the suggestion is to move you to a quality-control department. If you are a person who likes to push the boundaries and create new things, the conversation would indicate your reluctance to work in a group whose main task is essentially rule enforcement. However, if you firmly believe in rules-based order, this moral value would reveal itself through a happy face and a positive tone in the conversation.

The bottom line here is that our moral values direct our actions in response to surprises when there isn't much time to think and analyze the situation. Donald Calne, a neurologist and the author of *Within Reason*[133], makes this point by the following frequently quoted sentence: "The essential difference between emotion and reason is that emotion leads to action while reason leads to conclusions."[134,135]

We do act emotionally when there is no time to think, but reason and decisions still matter. We have plenty of time to decide what to learn and how to change our synapses, so that we embed holistic moral values in our mindset. In other words, we can utilize the brain plasticity to create neural paths for subconscious reactions that are not only quick but also consistent with the holistic effect of creating more for everyone. If we do it, we don't need to learn how to inhibit our actions; after all, lack of action is rarely helpful in the long term. If holistic moral values guide our emotional reactions, we will not regret them—quite the opposite, these will be emotionally-intelligent reactions with a positive impact. This is the premise for our discussion in this chapter.

We have discussed in previous chapters how enlightened self-interest creates holistic groups. In this chapter, we will focus on three specific moral values underlying the umbrella concept of enlightened self-interest.

Skepticism can be an emotionally intelligent moral value.

You are not helping others if you fail to protect yourself. In terms of interpersonal relationships, your first self-protection tool is skepticism.

Take as an example IBM's information about security breaches experienced in 2013 by its clients worldwide. According to their Cyber Security Intelligence Index, "more than half a billion records—including names, emails, credit card numbers, and passwords—were stolen," costing these companies more than $70 billion in total.[136] A common attack path exploits the emotions of email recipients by phishing. The attacker designs the email so as to look like it's coming from a reputable organization. For example, when the receiver sees a familiar company logo, the aim is to condition the receiver's brain and to remove any initial doubt. In the terminology we use in this book, they want you to generalize this similarity and, effectively, to ignore any differences from what would be a genuine email from the purported organization. However, this similarity is no reason to abandon your skepticism. The message in the phishing text will evoke an emotion, either fear or happiness, and it's far less likely you'll click on the offered link if you skeptically process the information available in the received email.

Specifically, processing information skeptically means not to be overwhelmed by portrayed similarities. This is the necessary mindset to initiate thinking by spotting and then analyzing suspicious differences. As illustrated in Chapter 5, the decision what to do with an observed difference is often obvious. In this example, spotting any characters or words beyond the usual email address will be a sure sign the email is a scam. To deal with other suspicious differences, you may need to make inquiries, but in this example you have the time to do it. If the email requests an immediate action, a skeptical brain will not see any immediate danger and its neural signals will ward the fingers off the requested mouse-click.

Adopting skepticism as your defensive moral value means you are building barriers in your brain to block unnecessary automatic actions, so that you don't end up ignoring relevant differences. In the phishing example, the aim is to block the emotional signals of either fear or happiness and to prevent the subconscious mouse-click on the offered link. Instead, the neural barriers should channel the new information into the thinking brain.

Coming from the Greek *skepticos*, meaning "thoughtful," the deep meaning of the word "skeptic" is an inquiring and reflective person. For the sake of your self-defense, you should adopt this meaning and reject the modern misconceptions of this concept. The Skeptic Society, a nonprofit scientific and educational organization with Dr Michael Shermer as its Executive Director, provides more detailed description:

> Some people believe that skepticism is the rejection of new ideas, or worse, they confuse "skeptic" with "cynic" and think that skeptics are a bunch of grumpy curmudgeons unwilling to accept any claim that challenges the status quo. This is wrong. Skepticism is a provisional

approach to claims. It is the application of reason to any and all ideas—no sacred cows allowed. In other words, skepticism is a method, not a position. Ideally, skeptics do not go into an investigation closed to the possibility that a phenomenon might be real or that a claim might be true. When we say we are "skeptical," we mean that we must see compelling evidence before we believe.[137]

This is the opposite from the common advice to give the benefit of the doubt in the absence of compelling evidence. According to this school of thought, doubt without a solid evidence leads to mistrust and possibly relationship breakdown.

Here is an example to elucidate the possible outcomes of these two contrasting approaches. Mr. Williams runs a small business, its main product being a patented sensor device. He is selling this product to a single large company, but he is doing well financially thanks to a very healthy margin between the sales price of $300 and the production cost. The large company, whose CEO is Mr. Clarke, benefits from the patented feature of the sensor device by building and selling a unique product to a growing number of customers.

One day, Clarke meets Williams to discuss a report about reliability issues with the sensor device. Clarke begins the meeting with a common phrase, "I have bad and good news." The bad news is that his engineers have traced customer complaints to reliability issues with the sensor device. The good news is that his engineers could design a workaround, which would add cost, but they are happy to move ahead with the new design if Williams could reduce the price of the sensor device to $200.

This supply deal has been the only source of income for Williams's company. Their attempts to diversify the client base are at the stage of negotiating a deal with a start-up company that can also pay no more than $200. Now, Williams is facing a considerable uncertainty as a result of Clarke's information about the reliability issues.

According to the don't-be-skeptical school of thought, Williams has no reason to doubt the information about reliability issues and he should accept Clarke's offer. Otherwise, he will be taking the risk of losing the existing sales and all income will dry out if he doesn't close the deal with the start-up company.

However, Williams may be facing what is called the dark side of emotional intelligence.[138] Clarke's bad and good news could be an attempt to manage Williams's emotions—the bad news scaring him with the potential of losing the sales, and then the good news making him feel happy about the option of reducing the price from $300 to $200.

Williams doesn't have any evidence that Clarke is engaging in this kind of emotional manipulation. However, he is a person who doesn't believe in highly-consequential actions without compelling evidence. This skepticism subdues both the fear due to the bad news and the happiness due to the good news. Williams needs evidence to believe what he has heard, and he asks for specific information about the reliability issue. Clarke pulls out an executive summary of the mentioned reliability analysis, but the summary provides no more than generic statements. For Williams, this is a reason to doubt and he asks for the reliability analysis with specific data. The meeting ends with Clarke saying he would see with his engineers whether he could provide the requested information.

This outcome leaves Williams in a much better position than if he acted emotionally to accept the price reduction. If Clarke does provide specific data, his engineers would be able to analyze the issue and, based on the results, they may be able to resolve the issue by modifying the sensor device. This would be far more favorable for their business opportunities in the future than to rely on Clarke's expensive workaround at the system level.

In the absence of the requested data, Williams can keep waiting by taking the business-as-usual approach. He can ignore the generic statements about reliability issues as he continues to negotiate with the start-up company. Regarding the future relationship with Clarke's company, Williams can see all their possible actions and he already knows how to respond to each of them. If Clarke calls for more discussions, he will engage for as long as he can see more transparency and progress toward a resolution of the issue. If they remain silent about the reliability problem but continue ordering devices at $300, he will continue with the sales. The final option is no further communication and no further orders. According to this scenario, Clarke would decide to lose a profitable business without giving Williams's engineers an opportunity to respond. This would signal either incompetence in Clarke's company or that they were playing on the dark side of emotional intelligence. Either way, it's better for Williams to cut his losses than to compromise his product and company image by maintaining such a risky and possibly deceitful engagement.

By asking for specific data, Williams has acted in response to the news about reliability issues—he did not ignore this negative feedback. In general, skepticism is not about rejecting negative feedback. As mentioned in Chapter 5, it hurts when you hear negative feedback without specific instructions of what to change. Nonetheless, some negative feedback cannot be delivered with instructions for adequate changes. In the example with the reliability issue, Clarke's company should be able to provide specific data about the observed problem, but they didn't invent the sensor device so they don't know what changes may or may not be possible at the device level. Williams's company would need to analyze the technical feedback—if they receive it—to see if they could change something to improve their invention.

The proper mindset regarding negative feedback is to think about changes in the future rather than try to change the past. Assuming Williams receives the technical information, his skeptical mind will neither reject the data nor accept the idea that the device is unfixable. However, an optimist may focus on the fact that the sensor device worked well for a long time and ignore the troublesome data. This selection of facts from the past may relieve the emotional pain, but it's unhelpful in the long term. On the other hand, it doesn't help to be a pessimist who drowns in the negative aspects of past events. The best approach is to accept what happened in the past but, as discussed in Chapters 2 and 6, distinguish these facts from their inherent interpretations in any decision about future actions.

Turning to positive feedback, skepticism is again about paying attention to and dealing with differences, if any. For example, skeptics don't need to subdue their happiness when deciding to buy something important. If a real-estate agent works out what a buyer needs and comes back with the news about a house ticking all the boxes, the lack of difference from the buyer's criteria is the reason for rational happiness. The decision to buy is emotional but—satisfying all thought through and set up criteria in advance—it's also rational. In this example, the seller properly employs his or her emotional intelligence to make the buyer happy and, hence, to close the purchase deal. On the other hand, if an emotionally-intelligent seller utilizes happiness due to a single feature to sell a house that doesn't satisfy key criteria, then the buyer needs skepticism as protection against this emotional manipulation.

Another buying-and-selling example can illustrate that a skeptical analysis can render a hyped difference as irrelevant. In 1975, the US Congress was debating a bill to outlaw a practice by credit-card companies to ban their affiliated stores from charging higher prices for purchases by credit cards. Unable to derail the bill, the credit-card lobby requested that "any difference between credit card and cash customers take the form of a cash discount rather than a credit card surcharge."[139] A skeptic can see that the one-dollar difference between a credit-card payment of $99 and a cash payment of $98 is the same, irrespective of whether it's labeled as either cash discount or credit-card surcharge. However, the credit-card companies made the right judgment that most customers would see a surcharge as penalty, creating emotional discouragement from using credit cards. This customer behavior illustrates the lack of habit to check whether an apparent difference is real or not.

Recognizing and tolerating uniqueness is a key step toward enlightened self-interest.

Recall the example of workers in Ford Motor Company when the mass production model turned them into menial operators. Easily replaceable, these humans turned into identical operators and indistinguishable cost items in the equations for cost and profit calculations. To an extent, managers see many of us as items in their financial spreadsheets. The difference in our modern times is that we are able to live lives with personal dignity, in the center of our own worlds. We are all different and we can enjoy our uniqueness.

It's natural to see yourself in the center of your own world. However, what's necessary here is to think about the perspective of others. How do you feel when an assessment panel rejects your project proposal, or a colleague receives promotion and a salary increase for the same job responsibilities? If you are angry, you are seeing yourself as equal if not better than the successful people. Yet the assessment panel and the promotion committee can always demonstrate that your case was different. Their point of view is different from yours. Unless you recognize this fact, you won't be able to see the reason for the unfavorable decisions and your anger will not help. Of course, this doesn't mean you should agree with the criteria for these decisions once you see the situation from the perspective of the decision makers. However, you will have the proper information to think about your future actions.

Dealing with envy is another example to show how recognizing uniqueness can help. A character who successfully resists the dark temptations of envy appears in the first chapter of Nassim Nicholas Taleb's book, *Fooled by Randomness*.[140] Nero Tulip is a fictional character, but his values are as real as their resemblance to Taleb's own character. In a nutshell, Nero is a risk-averse proprietary trader with a PhD degree and love for statistics and philosophy. In his job, he trades company's capital and enjoys the benefits of self-employment without "the boredom of running the mundane details of his own business."[141] Nero is not as rich as others in his position because he is a skeptic who doesn't invest his own money outside the safety of treasury bonds. On average, he makes $500,000 a year in after-tax money. Based on this income, enjoyable work, and fulfilling hobbies, it seems Nero has everything he wanted to have in his life. However, in comparison to his neighbor, he is missing a lot.

His neighbor, John, is a different character. John is much younger than Nero, but as a high-yield trader he is doing markedly better. John and his wife have a much larger house, with two prestige German cars, a collectible Ferrari, and another convertible parked on the driveway. Taleb describes the impact of neighbors' boasting by the following sentences:

> Nero's wife is all too human; although she kept telling herself that she did not want to be in the shoes of John's wife, she felt as she had been somewhat swamped in the competition of life. Somehow words and reason became ineffectual in front of an oversized diamond, a monstrous house, and a sports car collection.[142]

Trying to soothe his own envy, Nero read about the psychology of pecking order. According to the results of some studies, he would be happier with a smaller house if the neighboring houses were even smaller; in John's neighborhood, he needs a much bigger house.

However, Nero was skeptical about the long-term viability of John's success. To be able to compete fairly with John, he would need to abandon his risk-averse value and to undertake high-yield trading. With his background in statistics and understanding of high-yield markets, he knew that high-yield traders make big money every month for a long time only to lose a multiple of the accumulated amount in hours. Nero could see that taking the risk of such a big loss would mean risking his enjoyable job and lifestyle. Eventually, this is what happened to John when he ran out of his luck. He not only was fired but also lost almost everything he had.

The key point here is not about waiting for vindication, which may never happen. Tennis players don't lose their prize money, and yet we don't envy them. Roger Federer, one of the best tennis players of all time, collected the total of $100 million in prize money years ago, but people didn't envy him. To the contrary, his fans wanted to see him winning more money and increasing his lead on the scoreboard of won grand slams. We don't envy these people because they are so different from us. Nero and John are also different from one another, but the differences are much smaller and envy can overwhelm them. Yet these differences matter and it's easy for Nero to see them if he tries honestly to put himself in John's shoes. In his example, it's not enough to compare houses without a comparison of the values that—apart from luck—enabled John to have the large house and the sports car collection. Nero's life would be empty without books, which would be the case in John's shoes. Nero wouldn't like to swap his trading method and lifestyle with John. They are both traders, but they are not competing in the same game. The pecking order causing envy is due to flawed comparisons, and Nero wouldn't be true to his values if he adopts big houses and expensive cars as the exclusive measure of success and satisfaction in life.

Making comparisons is a fundamental scientific method, but flawed comparisons lead to wrong conclusions. An example is the comparison of abstract people in the so-called trolley dilemma. In the dominant view of professionals, this thought experiment allows them "to think through the consequences of an action and consider whether its moral value is determined solely by its outcome."[143] Here is the text of the trolley dilemma, as published in a philosophical paper in 1976:

Edward is the driver of a trolley, whose brakes have just failed. On the track ahead of him are five people; the banks are so steep that they will not be able to get off the track in time. The track has a spur leading off to the right, and Edward can turn the trolley onto it. Unfortunately there is one person on the right-hand track. Edward can turn the trolley, killing the one; or he can refrain from turning the trolley, killing the five.[144]

Most people say Edward should turn the trolley, although a minority of professionals don't give an answer. The ethics of sacrificing one individual to save five others makes sense if we don't see a problem with counting people's lives as mathematical units. To accept the mere number of lives as the relevant ethical gauge is to ignore the reality that different people could make vastly different contributions. Just think of the possibility that the five saved people were theorists plotting to kill hundreds. Alternatively, the person on the right-hand truck could've been someone with an idea to save millions of lives by developing a cure for a devastating disease. It's unethical to ignore differences between people. This popular thought experiment is abstract and misleading because it ignores these differences.

Moreover, the search for one correct answer to this and

other similar dilemmas inherently assumes that all people should have equal moral values. This disregard of diversity is a common trap for professionals who are prone to overgeneralizations. In Chapter 7, we discussed the choice between the certainty of taking $400 or tossing a coin for the chance to win either $1,000 or nothing. Both choices can be rational in different circumstances, but this reality is at odds with the philosophy of one rational answer.

The belief in the idea of one correct answer for moral dilemmas leads to intolerance for diverse views. A report by the Skeptic Research Center about moral attitudes and political intolerance provides an example. According to the reported study, the most intolerant group were more likely to agree that (1) the US government should provide financial support to people in other countries, (2) the US government should open its borders to all immigrants in need, and (3) political conflict is a major threat to society. Calling the findings a "paradox of tolerance," the researchers described the paradox by the following words: "... people most willing to extend aid to those in *other* societies are also most irritated by political disagreements with those living in *their own* society."[145]

The root of intolerance in this example is the view of these people that everyone should share their moral values. Yet not only countries but also companies and even teams need diversity. So we don't need these irritated people to tell us what each of us should think. What we need are safe, fair, and favorable conditions for each of us to try our own ideas for prosperity while not endangering others.

In companies, the management sets rules for safety and creates conditions for development of employees. They enforce the rules and encourage development by punishment and rewards. When assessing employees' performance and setting conditions for their development, good managers recognize diversity. Others try to make objective decisions by strict adherence to key performance indicators (KPIs). A problem with the idea of objective KPIs is the tendency to set numerical criteria to enable objective comparisons between employees. In many cases this ignores unique but important contributions of different people. For example, if a manager compares people by the number of hours they sit in front of a computer, or by the number of pages they type, the manager will increase the number of typed pages at the expense of quality analyses and original thinking.

A final note about the value of recognizing uniqueness and diversity is a warning not to overgeneralize these concepts. A good example for this point is education. There are too many random ways to try unique things and they typically don't work, or are even dangerous. Adults teach their children not to put poisonous stuff in their mouth and not to inspect power sockets with metal pins. Nonetheless, people need to try their own ideas and to develop their individualities. The trick here is to create a safe envelope and to provide as useful advice as possible, but also to tolerate explorations by people who are inclined to learn by their own experiences. No matter how strongly we believe in our rules, we should remember what we've discovered at the beginning of this book: Individual atoms and molecules don't follow strictly the rigid rules of physics, so we shouldn't expect the complex human brains to follow strict trajectories professed by their educators or leaders. However, when we set the right conditions, we know that most of the jiggling atoms will find their stable positions in the crystal we wish to grow, just as roaming molecules find their pairs in the process of gene replication. Likewise, the wandering minds rediscover things others have known for a long time, albeit with necessary adaptations to match their individuality.

Giving has value for personal benefit.

Going back to the question of whether a developed country should accept all immigrants in need, the available evidence is that most people are against this idea if they don't see a benefit for their country.

Denmark is one of the richest countries in Europe, proud of human rights standards, equality, and social welfare.[146] In 2015, millions of refugees were arriving from the Middle East to seek asylum in the countries of Western Europe. In response to the majority of Danish voters, who didn't think uncontrolled immigration could benefit their country, the government introduced strict asylum rules.

A study on voter responses to diversity and migration in high-income democracies found similar attitude ahead of the Brexit referendum, the 2016 referendum on the departure of United Kingdom from the European Union.[147] The study found that only 12 percent of respondents were "global altruists," willing to relax existing restrictions in principle. However, 58 percent said they were willing to do it "for those immigrants who would contribute to the national economy." The author of the study calls this effect "parochial altruism," but this is just looking at enlightened self-interest from the philosophical perspective of altruism.

The parochial effect becomes more pronounced in smaller and more cohesive groups, such as employees in a company. Furthermore, at the level of small teams, the criterion for acceptance of new people is even higher and may conflict with the self-interest of some members of the team. Assume your team is discussing the need to appoint an additional person with similar skills to yours. The first instinct might be to see the new employee as a competitor. Your reaction in this situation will show whether your moral values are holistic.

In the scenario when you are unable to see well-presented benefits for the team, you will be also ignorant of your own benefits. Anger will convey your preparedness to fight in defense of your exclusive position in the team. In that case, your self-interest is shortsighted and destructive for the team and for yourself. You need an understanding of the holistic principle to shift your mindset from shortsighted to enlightened self-interest.

Of course, it may turn out that the proposal is not good for the team. However, you don't know this instantly and allowing anger to drive your response is unhelpful. Skepticism rather than anger is a good first-defense tool. With skepticism you'll begin to think about the new situation and you'll ask questions to understand how adding another employee in your area might help the team. Asking these questions will disclose your skepticism, but you are on safe ground in comparison to displaying preparedness to fight for control of your patch. If the person proposing the new appointment responds to your skepticism by attacking you rather than answering the questions, there is no need to retreat. When people ask you to do something and disrespect you by refusing to explain how they see the benefits and the risks, the safe response is to exercise your free will and say "no."

In the previous examples, we focused the concept of *giving for personal benefit* on the effects of giving away unconditional control and allowing other people to enter your territory. Let's now take a look at the potential personal benefits when someone gives away material possessions. To use money as the best example, recall that the development of penicillin drug started in 1938—ten years after Alexander Fleming discovered in 1928 that *Penicillium* mold kills bacteria. Many rich people donated money to various charities during these ten years. Imagine a wealthy individual ends up in a hospital in 1938 with a bacterial infection. The person could pay a lot of money to buy any number of the most expensive medications, but the drug to cure the fatal infection is not available. The situation could've been different if the money was offered ten years earlier and the penicillin drug was developed earlier. Of course, there was neither certainty that the person would need the drug nor certainty that the drug development would be successful. This uncertainty makes giving different from buying.

The certain personal benefit from giving away money or other possessions is the feeling of satisfaction and even happiness. The positive feelings are stronger when we give to people closer to us, or help people in greater need, or donate for a cause we are passionate about. When that's not the case, the positive emotions are still beneficial if a person can give something without conflicting negative feelings.

Finally, let's focus on the personal benefits of giving away knowledge. Again, we are not talking here about the useful knowledge that people sell and buy in a variety of ways, such as training, books, patents, and so on. The context is again uncertainty and the focus is on giving knowledge to improve our chances for a personal benefit.

A typical example is the ideas of academics in the course of doing their research. These new ideas have random elements and they usually don't work in the initial form. Regardless, many academics focus on the promising aspects and prefer to keep them secret as their own seed knowledge. However, others are happy to share such ideas with their colleagues. Apart from this instant satisfaction, they also create a much better chance for the idea to evolve into usable knowledge. They will have to share the benefit of the eventual success, but sharing something tangible is obviously better than the exclusive ownership of a useless idea.

When an idea is developed to the level known as proof of concept, and perhaps patented, the inventor needs investment to commercialize it. Investors know that taking technologies or methods from their inventors could be as counterproductive as trying to snatch a baby from a mother.

Here is a specific example of a meeting among a technology inventor, prospective investors, and other parties interested in the potential commercialization of a new technology. During the meeting, one of the attendees asked the others to think of a recognizable name for the technology. A few minutes later, the key investor floats the idea of using the inventor's name as the trademark. This surprises the inventor and excites his ego. But his holistic moral value is to maximize the opportunity for commercialization by attracting and motivating others to make their contributions. Driven by this moral value, the inventor responds by suggesting the use of a different name to associate the technology trademark with the company brand. This emotional reaction is a sure signal that the inventor is giving away his control of the technology for the sake of its successful commercialization.

To conclude, we highlight the importance of this moral value by the following two sentences: The ability to share ideas and work together to reshape them into new knowledge has enabled the fast evolution and the incredible progress of our human society. We need to continue sharing diverse and contestable ideas to survive and prosper in the future, for we know that the future will be different from the past.

Acknowledgements

This book wouldn't happen without my co-author, Maryann Karinch. As I write in the Author's Note, we employed our complementary skills and expertise with the common motivation to help people with the challenges in our uncertain world. Working with Maryann, I've also learned how to write for the general audience—a huge leap from the writing style of academics. For this, I am enormously grateful.

My thinking about work and life has evolved through countless interactions and discussions with other people, including colleagues, project partners, students, and friends in our bunch of first-generation immigrants. They are too many to list individually, but I acknowledge their profound impact on my learning through life. I've also gained valuable insights and learned a lot from the closest but much younger people than me: Oskar and Olivia in the youngest row, with Milan, Mirjana, and Jason as the intermediate generation. For more than half of my life, I've shared almost every day of my journey with my wife Vesna—no words are sufficient to express my gratitude for her support and impact on my life experience.

--Sima

Sima came to me with scintillating concepts and I am thrilled to have worked with him to bring them to a general audience. I am very grateful to him for trusting me to serve as his partner in producing this book.

Thank you to Joe McNeely at Brilliance Audio for seeing how valuable this book could be to a general business audience. Your faith in our work has been inspiring.

Thanks to Judith Bailey for taking on this project at Armin Lear. We also appreciate the great creative talents of Casey and Emily Fritz at Albatross Design Co., with Casey designing the cover and Emily arranging our words on the pages. I have enjoyed working with all of you!

Thank you also to Jim McCormick, always a great source of support, keen insights, and patience. And, of course, I thank my Mom and my Brother Karl for being in my corner and encouraging me always.

--Maryann

Author Bios

Sima Dimitrijev is a Professor at Griffith University in Australia. He is an educator, a microelectronic engineer, a researcher, an inventor, and the author of two textbooks. Sima has led many research and development projects, funded by industry, governments, and venture-capital investors. In addition to the textbooks on semiconductor devices, published by Oxford University Press, New York, and translated into Korean and Chinese, he has published over 180 papers in peer-reviewed journals and many papers in conference proceedings. According to the "Google Scholar" database, these papers were cited more than 5,800 times by authors of other papers. Sima's peer-reviewed papers appeared in more than 40 different journals, many of them publishing seemingly disconnected areas of scholarship—from crystal growth to cognitive memory networks and intelligent systems. This unusual spread of scholarship across different areas of expertise matches the unique depth that *Trial, Error, and Success* seeks to convey.

Sima received BEng, MSci, and PhD degrees in Electronic Engineering from the University of Nis, in 1982, 1985, and 1989, respectively. From 1982 to 1983, he was with the Semiconductor Factory, Electronics Industry, Nis, working on development of CMOS technology. From 1983 to 1990, he was with the Faculty of Electronic Engineering at University of Nis. In 1990, he joined Griffith University. He is a member of the Editorial Advisory Board, Microelectronics Reliability, Elsevier/Pergamon, and a Senior Member of IEEE.

Maryann Karinch is the author of articles, books, and white papers including 33 commercially published books and more than 200 published articles. A blogger for Psychology Today, she is also the ghostwriter of 8 books. Maryann has trained law/code enforcement professionals, corporate audiences, and psychology and business students in interpersonal skills and serves as an expert for media on reading and using body language. She holds a BA and MA from The Catholic University of America, Washington, DC. Maryann has been certified since 1998 by the American Council on Exercise as a personal trainer and is a member of The Authors Guild and The Explorers Club.

Books Authored

Trial, Error, and Success (co-author Sima Dimitrijev, PhD, Armin Lear Press, Brilliance Audio, 2021)

Cosmic Careers (co-author Alastair Browne, HarperCollins Leadership, 2021)

Get People to Do What You Want (2nd) (co-author Gregory Hartley, Career Press/Red Wheel Weiser, 2019)

Mature Sexual Intimacy (Rowman & Littlefield, July 2019)

Control the Conversation (co-author James O. Pyle, Career Press/ Red Wheel Weiser, 2018)

Deepwater Deception (co-author Robert Kaluza, Armin Lear, 2018)

Basic Wilderness Survival Skills (update of the classic by Bradford Angier, Globe Pequot Press, 2018)

Body Language Sales Secrets (co-author Jim McCormick, Career Press/ Red Wheel Weiser, 2017)

Sex and Cancer: Intimacy, Love, and Romance after Diagnosis and Treatment (co-author Saketh Guntupalli, MD, Rowman & Littlefield, Spring 2017)

The Art of Body Talk (co-author Gregory Hartley, Career Press, 2017)

Blending Families (co-author Trevor Crow Mullineaux, LMFT, Rowman & Littlefield, 2016)

The Vaccination Debate (co-author Christopher Spinelli, D.O., New Horizon Press, 2015)

Government of ALL the People (co-author Robert L. Saloschin, Armin Lear, 2015)

Nothing But the Truth (Career Press, 2015)

Find Out Anything from Anyone, Anytime (co-author James O. Pyle, Career Press, 2014)

Forging Healthy Connections (co-author Trevor Crow, LMFT, New Horizon Press, 2013)

The Wandering Mind (co-author John A. Biever, MD, Rowman & Littlefield, 2012)

The Most Dangerous Business Book You'll Ever Read (co-author Gregory Hartley, Wiley & Sons, 2011)

Business Confidential (co-author Peter Earnest, HarperCollins, 2010)

The Body Language Handbook (co-author Gregory Hartley, Career Press, 2010)

Business Lessons from the Edge (co-author Jim McCormick, McGraw-Hill, 2009)

365 Ways to Get a Good Night's Sleep (co-author Ronald L. Kotler, MD, DABSM, Adams Media, 2009)

Get People to Do What You Want (co-author Gregory Hartley, Career Press, 2008)

Date Decoder (co-author Gregory Hartley, Adams Media, 2008)

How to Become an Expert on Anything in Two Hours (co-author Gregory Hartley, AMACOM, 2008)

Empowering Underachievers (co-author Dr. Peter Spevak, New Horizon Press, 2000 and 2006)

How to Spot a Liar (co-author Gregory Hartley, Career Press, 2005 and 2010)

Dr. David Sherer's Hospital Survival Guide (co-author David Sherer, MD, Claren Books, 2003)

Rangers Lead the Way (co-author Dean Hohl, Adams Media, 2003)
Diets Designed for Athletes (Human Kinetics, 2001)
Lessons from the Edge (Simon & Schuster, 2000)
Boot Camp (co-author Patrick "The Sarge" Avon, Simon &
     Schuster, 1999)
Telemedicine: What the Future Holds When You're Ill (New Horizon
     Press, 1994)

Endnotes

1   N.N. Taleb, *Fooled by Randomness: The Hidden Role of Chance in Life and in the Markets*, 2nd Edition (New York: Random House, 2005).

2   N.M. Ferguson, D. Laydon, G. Nedjati-Gilani, N. Imai, K. Ainslie, M. Baguelin, S. Bhatia, A. Boonyasiri, Z. Cucunubá, G. Cuomo-Dannenburg, and A. Dighe, "Impact of non-pharmaceutical interventions (NPIs) to reduce COVID-19 mortality and healthcare demand. Imperial College COVID-19," Response Team, London, March 16, 2020; https://www.imperial.ac.uk/media/imperial-college/medicine/sph/ide/gida-fellow-ships/Imperial-College-COVID19-NPI-modelling-16-03-2020.pdf

3   Richard Feynman, *What Do You Care What Other People Think?* (New York: WW Norton Co., 2018).

4   P.S. Laplace, *A Philosophical Essay on Probabilities* (New York: John Wiley & Sons, 1902), p. 4.

5   R. Lewontin, "Genes, organisms and environment", in *Evolution from Molecules to Man*, D. S. Bendall, Editor (Cambridge, UK: Cambridge University Press, 1983).

6   M. Born, *Experiment and Theory in Physics*, (New York: Cambridge University Press, 1943), p. 44.

7   R. Feynman, *The Character of Physical Law*, (Cambridge, MA: MIT Press, 1967), p. 156.

8   A. Wagner, *Arrival of the Fittest: How Nature Innovates*, (New York, Current, 2015).

9   P. Thiel with B. Masters, *Zero to One: Notes on Startups, or How to Build the Future,* (New York: Crown Business, 2014); p. 146.

10   https://twitter.com/elonmusk/status/984882630947753984

11   http://www.hitachi.com/rd/portal/highlight/quantum/doubleslit/index.html

12   M. Twain, "The Lowest Animal," in *Mark Twain Letters from the Earth*, Bernard DeVoto, Editor (New York: Harper & Row, 1962), pp. 222–232.

13   *Ibid.*

14   M. Born, *My Life and Views* (New York: Charles Scribner, 1968), p. 183.

15   *On 1984: Quotes for the Orwellian Future Happening Today*, James Daley, Editor (New York: Racehorse Publishing, 2017).

16   J.D. Stein, *Cosmic Numbers: The Numbers that Define Our Universe* (New York: Basic Books, 2011), p. 103.

17   https://www.huffingtonpost.com/brett-berry/why-was-5-x-3-5-5-5-marked-wrong_b_8468722.html

18   *The Born–Einstein Letters: Correspondence between Albert Einstein and Max and Hedwig Born from 1916 to 1955*, with commentaries by Max Born, translated by Irene Born (London: Macmillan, 1971), p. 149.

19   G.C. Ainsworth, "Agostino Bassi, 1773–1856," Nature, vol. 177, pp. 255–257, 1956.

20   K. Newman, *Macmillan, Khrushchev and the Berlin Crisis, 1958–1960* (Abingdon, Oxon: Routledge, 2007), p. 177.

21   C. Orzel, "What sorts of problems are quantum computers good for?", *Forbes*, April 17, 2017; https://www.forbes.com/sites/chadorzel/2017/04/17/what-sorts-of-problems-are-quantum-computers-good-for/

22   J. Whalen, "The quantum revolution is coming, and Chinese scientists are at the forefront," *Washington Post*, April 19, 2019; https://www.washingtonpost.com/business/2019/08/18/quantum-revolution-is-coming-chinese-scientists-are-forefront/

23   J. Gribbin, "The paradox of Schrödinger's waves", *New Scientist*, pp. 37–39, 27 Aug. 1987 (p. 39).

24   S. Cohen, "The real reason behind NY Governor Andrew Cuomo's surprising confession," *Forbes*, May 26, 2020; https://www.forbes.com/sites/sethcohen/2020/05/26/we-all-failed--the-real-reason-behind-ny-governor-andrew-cuomos-surprising-confession/

25   J.P. Womack and D.T. Jones, *Lean Thinking: Banish Waste and Create Wealth in Your Corporation* (New York: Simon & Schuster, 1996).

26   J.P. Womack and D.T. Jones, "Lean consumption," *Harvard Business Review,* March 2005, pp. 58—68.

27   P. Kosky et al, *Exploring Engineering: An Introduction to Engineering and Design*, 4th Edition (Amsterdam: Academic Press, 2015).

28   S. Dimitrijev, "Are laws of nature discovered or invented? Continuous change, discrete events, and the nature of reality", *Skeptic*, vol. 25, No. 4, pp. 54–56, 2020.

29   S. Hawking, *Brief Answers to the Big Questions* (New York: Bantam, 2018).

30   E. Mack, "Stephen Hawking believed time travel was more likely than the existence of God," *Forbes*, October 16, 2018

31   White House, October 5, 2016; https://obamawhitehouse.archives. gov/the-press-office/2016/10/05/remarks-president-paris-agreement

32   M. Gladwell, *Outliers: The Story of Success* (New York: Little, Brown and Company, 2008).

33   N.N. Taleb, *The Black Swan: The Impact of the Highly Improbable*, 2nd Edition (New York: Random House, 2010).

34   L. Tolstoy, *Anna Karenina*, translated by C. Garnett (New York: Random House, 2000).

35   J. Diamond, *Guns, Germs, and Steel: The Fates of Human Societies* (New York: W.W. Norton, 1997).

36   R. Dawkins, *The Selfish Gene*, 2nd Edition (Oxford: Oxford University Press, 1990).

37   P. Thiel with B. Masters, *Zero to One: Notes on Startups, or How to Build the Future* (New York: Crown Business, 2014), p. 34.

38   A.D. Chandler, Jr., ed. *Giant Enterprise: Ford, General Motors, and the Automobile Industry* (New York: Harcourt, Brace, & World, 1964), p. 28.

39   D. Gartman, "Harley Earl and the art and color section: The birth of styling at General Motors," in *Design History: An Anthology*, D.P. Doordan, Editor (Cambridge, MA: MIT Press, 2000), p. 125.

40   R. M. Goodwin, "A growth cycle", in C.H. Feinstein, Editor, *Socialism, Capitalism and Economic Growth* (Cambridge: Cambridge University Press, 1967).

41   J. Schofield, "Ken Olsen obituary," *The Guardian*, February 10, 2011

42   A. Grove, *Only the Paranoid Survive: How to Exploit the Crisis Points That Challenge Every Company* (New York: Doubleday, 1996).

43   John F. Kennedy Speeches, Indianapolis, Indiana, April, 12, 1959, in John F. Kennedy Presidential Library and Museum; https://www.jfklibrary.org/Research/Research-Aids/JFK-Speeches/ Indianapolis-IN_19590412.aspx

44   W. James, *The Principles of Psychology*, vol. 2 (New York: Dover Publications, Republished Edition, 1950), p. 330.

45   S. Selvin, "A problem in probability," *The American Statistician*, vol. 29, p. 67, 1975.

46   M. vos Savant, *The Power of Logical Thinking: Easy Lessons in the Art of Reasoning... and Hard Facts About Its Absence in Our Lives* (New York: St Martin's Griffin, 1997), p. 6.

47   M. vos Savant, "Game show problem"; http://marilynvossavant.com/game-show-problem/

48   D. Kahneman, *Thinking, Fast and Slow* (New York: Farrar, Straus and Giroux, 2011).

49   R.H. Thaler and C.R. Sunstein, *Nudge: Improving Decisions about Health, Wealth, and Happiness* (New York: Penguin, 2009).

50   W.T. Herbranson and J. Schroeder, "Are birds smarter than mathematicians? Pigeons (Columba livia) perform optimally on a version of the Monty Hall dilemma," *Journal of Comparative Psychology*, vol. 124, pp. 1-13, 2010.

51   A. Fleming, "The discovery of penicillin," *British Medical Bulletin*, vol. 2, pp. 4-5, 1944.

52   R. Gaynes, "The Discovery of Penicillin—New Insights After More Than 75 Years of Clinical Use," *Emerging Infectious Diseases*, vol. 23, pp. 849-853, 2017.

53   A. Fleming, "On the antibacterial action of cultures of a Penicillium with special reference to their use in the isolation of B. influenza," *British Journal of Experimental Pathology*, vol. 10, pp. 226-36, 1929.

54   American Chemical Society International Historic Chemical Landmarks. Discovery and Development of Penicillin; http://www.acs.org/content/acs/en/education/whatischemistry/landmarks/flemingpenicillin.html

55   *Ibid.*

56   M. Asano et al, "Inhibitory effects of w-3 polyunsaturated fatty acids on receptor-mediated non-selective cation currents in rat A7r5 vascular smooth muscle cells, *British Journal of Pharmacology* vol. 120, pp. 1367-1375, 1997.

57   C. Moreno *et al*, "Effects of *n*-3 polyunsaturated fatty acids on cardiac ion channels," *Frontiers in Physiology*, vol. 3, pp. 245-1-245-8, 2012.

58   T. Hoshi *et al*, "Omega-3 fatty acids lower blood pressure by directly activating large-conductance Ca2+-dependent K+ channels," *Proc. Natl. Acad. Sci. USA*, vol. 110, pp. 4816-4821, 2013; T. Hoshi *et al*, "Mechanism of the modulation of BK potassium channel complexes with different auxiliary subunit compositions by the omega-3 fatty acid DHA," *Proc. Natl. Acad. Sci. USA*, vol. 110, pp. 4822-4827, 2013.

59   F. Elinder and S.I. Liin, "Actions and mechanisms of polyunsaturated fatty acids on voltage-gated ion channels," *Frontiers in Physiology*, vol. 8, pp. 43-1-43-24, 2017.

60   J.S. Hussein, "Cell membrane fatty acids and health," *International Journal of Pharmacy and Pharmaceutical Sciences*, vol 5, pp. 38-46, 2017.

61   M.E. Surette, "The science behind dietary omega-3 fatty acids," *Canadian Medical Association Journal*, vol. 178, pp. 177-180, 2008.

62   M. Schlosshauer, J. Kofler, and A. Zeilinger, "A snapshot of foundational attitudes toward quantum mechanics," pp. 222-230, 2013.

63   F.L. Dyer and T.C. Martin, *Edison: His Life and Inventions*, vol. 2 (New York: Harper & Brothers, 1910), pp. 615–616.

64   M. Gladwell, *Blink: The Power of Thinking without Thinking* (New York: Little, Brown and Company, 2005).

65   L. Mlodinow, *Subliminal: How Your Unconscious Mind Rules Your Behavior* (New York: Vintage, 2013).

66   R.H. Thaler and C.R. Sunstein, *Nudge: Improving Decisions about Health, Wealth, and Happiness* (New York: Penguin, 2009); pp. 19–20.

67   J.R. Hughes, *Physiological Reviews. 38 (1), 91–113, 1958.*

68   S.R. Howard *et al*, "Numerical cognition in honeybees enables addition and subtraction," *Science Advances*, vol. 5: eaav0961, pp. 1–6, 2019.

69   *In-flight upset 154 km west of Learmonth, WA; 7 October 2008; VH-QPA; Airbus 330-303* (Australian Transport Safety Bureau, 2011), p. 40

70   *Ibid*, p. 80.

71   Matt O'Sullivan, "The untold story of QF72: What happens when 'psycho' automation leaves pilots powerless?", (Sydney Morning Herald, 12 May 2017;

72   M. Mitchell Waldrop, "Flying the Electric Skies," *Science*, vol. 244, pp. 1532–1534, 1989.

73   *Ibid.*

74   https://boeing.mediaroom.com/2011-08-30-Boeing-Launches-737-New-Engine-Family-with-Commitments-for-496-Airplanes-from-Five-Airlines

75   https://www.cbsnews.com/news/boeing-737-max-8-boeing-737-800-how-are-the-planes-different/

76   P.A. Roitsch, G.L. Babcock, and W.W. Edmunds, Human Factors Report on the Tenerife Accident (Washington, DC: Air Line Pilots Association), p. 24

77   *Ibid*, p. 12

78   Report on the accident involving aircraft BOEING 747 PH-BUF of KLM and BOEING 747 N 736 PA of PANAM (Madrid: Comision de accidents, 12 July 1978; http://www.project-tenerife.com/engels/PDF/Tenerife.pdf), p. 44

79   *Ibid*, p. 45

80   Dutch comments on the Spanish Report, http://www.project-tenerife.com/engels/PDF/Dutch_comments.PDF

81   https://www.acxiom.com/customer-data/predictive-audiences/audience-propensities/

82   D. Gelles, N. Kitroeff, J. Nicas, and R.R. Ruiz, "Boeing was 'Go, Go, Go' to beat Airbus with the 737 Max," *The New York Times*, March 23, 2019; https://www.nytimes.com/2019/03/23/business/boeing-737-max-crash.html

83   G. Travis, "How the Boeing 737 Max disaster looks to a software developer," *IEEE Spectrum*, April 19, 2019; https://spectrum.ieee.org/aerospace/aviation/how-the-boeing-737-max-disaster-looks-to-a-software-developer

84   J. Nicas, N. Kitroeff, D. Gelles, and J. Glanz, "Boeing built deadly assumptions into 737 Max, blind to a late design change," *New York Times*, June 1, 2019; https://www.nytimes.com/2019/06/01/business/boeing-737-max-crash.html

85   https://www.faa.gov/about/mission/

86   M. Laris, "Changes to flawed Boeing 737 Max were kept from pilots, DeFazio says," *Washington Post*, June 19, 2019; https://www.washingtonpost.com/local/trafficandcommuting/changes-to-flawed-boeing-737-max-were-kept-from-pilots-defazio-says/2019/06/19/553522f0-92bc-11e9-aadb-74e6b2b46f6a_story.html?noredirect=on&utm_term=.fd957abcca22

87   A. Bloch, *Murphy's Law Book Two: More Reasons Why Things Go Wrong*, (Los Angeles, CA: Price/Stern/Sloan Publishers, 1980), p. 52.

88   M. Grothe, 2011, *Neverisms: A Quotation Lover's Guide to Things You Should Never Do, Never Say, or Never Forget*, (New York: HarperCollins, 2011).

89   M. Laris, "Changes to flawed Boeing 737 Max were kept from pilots, DeFazio says," *Washington Post*, June 19, 2019; https://www.washingtonpost.com/local/trafficandcommuting/changes-to-flawed-boeing-737-max-were-kept-from-pilots-defazio-says/2019/06/19/553522f0-92bc-11e9-aadb-74e6b2b46f6a_story.html?noredirect=on&utm_term=.fd957abcca22

90   D. Kahneman and A. Tversky, "Prospect theory: An analysis of decision under risk," *Econometrica*, vol. 47, pp. 263–292, 1979.

91   A. Tversky, "A critique of expected utility theory: Descriptive and normative considerations," *Erkenntnis*, vol. 9, pp. 163–173, 1975.

92   I. Miladinovic, "Ko je bio Josip Broz Tito?," *Novi Standard*, May 4, 2020; https://www.standard.rs/2020/05/04/ko-je-bio-josip-broz/

93   R.H. Anderson, "Giant among communists governed like a monarch," Tito's Obituary, *New York Times*, May 5, 1980.

94   *Ibid.*

95   J. McCurry, "The last kamikaze: two Japanese pilots tell how they cheated death," *The Guardian*, August 11, 2015; https://www.theguardian.com/world/2015/aug/11/the-last-kamikaze-two-japanese-pilots-tell-how-they-cheated-death

96   L. Bock, *Work Rules!: Insights from Inside Google That Will Transform How You Live and Lead*, (New York: Twelve, 2015).

97   M. Peng and K. Meyer, *International Business*, 2nd Ed., (Andover, Hampshire, UK: Cengage Learning EMEA, 201, 2016), p. 49.

98   S. Meyer, *The Five Dollar Day: Labor Management and Social Control in the Ford Motor Company, 1908-1921* (Albany: State University of New York Press, 1981), p. 48.

99   Ford Motor Co. Press release announcing the five-dollar day, January 5, 1914; The Ford Archives, Dearborn, Michigan.

100   D.M.G. Raff and L.H. Summers, "Did Henry Ford pay efficiency wages?", *Journal of Labor Economics*, vol. 5, pp. S57–S86, 1987.

101   H. Ford, *My Life and Work,*. (Garden City, N.Y.: Doubleday, 1922), p. 127.

102   D.M.G. Raff and L.H. Summers, "Did Henry Ford pay efficiency wages?", *Journal of Labor Economics*, vol. 5, pp. S57–S86, 1987.

103   A. Nevins, *Ford: The Times, the Man, and the Company*, (New York: Scribner, 1954), p. 549.

104   D.M.G. Raff and L.H. Summers, "Did Henry Ford pay efficiency wages?", *Journal of Labor Economics*, vol. 5, pp. S57–S86, 1987.

105   M. Anderson, "Ford's five dollar day," *The Henry Ford*, January 3, 2014; https://www.thehenryford.org/explore/blog/fords-five-dollar-day/

106   L. Bloom and C. Bloom, "Enlightened self-interest: The ultimate self-interest lies in being good to others," *Psychology Today*, December 17, 2012; https://www.psychologytoday.com/au/blog/stronger-the-broken-places/201212/enlightened-self-interest

107   F.W Taylor, *The Principles of Scientific Management* (New York: Harper and Brothers, 1919)

108   E.H. Kessler, P.E. Bierly, III, and S. Gopalakrishnan, "Vasa syndrome: Insights from a 17th-century new-product disaster," *Academy of Management Executive*, vol. 15, pp. 80–91, 2001.

109   *Ibid.*

110   C. Darwin, *The Expression of the Emotions in Man and Animals* (London: John Murray, 1872).

111   M. Karinch, *Lessons from the Edge: Extreme Athletes Show You How to Take on High Risk and Succeed* (New York: Simon & Schuster, 2000), p. 217.

112   B.G. Levi, "Nobel Prize in Physics recognizes research leading to high-brightness blue LEDs," *Physics Today*, vol. 67, pp. 14–17, 2014; doi: 10.1063/PT.3.2606

113   I. Akasaki, "Fascinated journeys into blue light," Nobel Lecture, December 8, 2014; https://www.nobelprize.org/uploads/2018/06/akasaki-lecture.pdf

114   S. Nakamura, "Background story of the invention of efficient blue InGaN light emitting diodes," Nobel Lecture, December 8, 2014; https://www.nobelprize.org/uploads/2018/06/nakamura-lecture.pdf

115   A. Yang, "The story behind Shuji Nakamura's

invention of blue LEDs," *LEDinside*, October 14, 2014; https://www.ledinside.com/news/2014/10/the_story_behind_shuji_nakamuras_invention_of_blue_leds

116   T. Crow and M. Karinch, *Forging Healthy Connections* (Far Hills, New Jersey: New Horizon Press, 2013), p. 120.

117   N.S. Godfrey and T. Richards, *Making Change: A Woman's Guide to Designing Her Financial Future* (New York: Simon & Schuster, 1999), p. 191.

118   M. Twain, "More Maxims of Mark," in *Mark Twain: Collected Tales, Sketches, Speeches, & Essays, 1891–1910*, Ed. Louis J. Budd (Des Moines, IA: Library of America, 1992), p. 944.

119   M. Twain, *The Wit and Wisdom of Mark Twain: The Book of Quotations* (Mineola, NY: Dover Publications, 1999), p. 43.

120   D. Kahneman and A. Deaton, "High income improves evaluation of life but not emotional well-being," *Proc. Natl. Acad. Sci. USA*, vol. 107, pp. 16489–16493, 2010.

121   *Ibid.*

122   K. Weise, "The CEO paying everyone $70,000 salaries has something to hide: Inside the viral story of Gravity CEO Dan Price," *Bloomberg Businessweek*, December 1, 2015; https://www.bloomberg.com/features/2015-gravity-ceo-dan-price/

123   S. Rodrick, "The prophet motive: Is Dan Price a sinner or a savior?" *Esquire*, August 3, 2016; https://www.esquire.com/lifestyle/a46922/dan-price-the-prophet-motive-esq-2016/

124   T. Bishop, "Trial begins in Gravity Payments case as Price brothers dispute CEO pay and company control," *GeekWire*, May 31, 2016; https://www.geekwire.com/2016/gravity-payments-trial/

125   M. Weiss, M.I. Norton, M. Norris, and S. McAra. "The $70K CEO at Gravity Payments." *Harvard Business School Case 816-010*, August 2015.

126   S. Rodrick, "The prophet motive: Is Dan Price a sinner or a savior?" *Esquire*, August 3, 2016; https://www.esquire.com/lifestyle/a46922/dan-price-the-prophet-motive-esq-2016/

127   D. Price, *Worth It: How a Million-Dollar Pay Cut and a $70,000 Minimum Wage Revealed a Better Way of Doing Business* (Seattle: Gravity Payments, 2020).

128   S. Rodrick, "The prophet motive: Is Dan Price a sinner or a savior?" *Esquire*, August 3, 2016; https://www.esquire.com/lifestyle/a46922/dan-price-the-prophet-motive-esq-2016/

129   https://twitter.com/DanPriceSeattle/status/1297583024587104262

130   D. Forbes, "New evidence supports allegations that famed $70K CEO Dan Price beat ex-wife," *Hundred Eighty Degrees,* February 27, 2018; https://www.hundredeightydegrees.com/investigation/2018/2/27/70k-ceo-makes-a-mint-tortures-ex-wife-advises-on-metoo

131 D. Gilbert, *Stumbling on Happiness* (New York: Vintage Books, 2007).

132 P. Salovey, J.D. Mayer, "Emotional intelligence," *Imagination, Cognition and Personality*, vol. 9, pp. 185–211, 1990.

133 D. Calne, *Within Reason: Rationality and Human Behavior* (New York: Vintage, 2000).

134 L. Pinci and P. *Glosserman, Sell the Feeling: The 6-Step System That Drives People to Do Business with You* (Garden City, NY: Morgan James Publishing, 2008), p. VII.

135 K. Kompella, *The Definitive Book of Branding* (Los Angeles: Sage, 2014), p. 375.

136 IBM Security Services 2014 Cyber Security Intelligence Index; https://www.ibm.com/developerworks/library/se-cyberindex2014/index.html

137 https://www.skeptic.com/about_us/

138 M. Kilduff, D.S. Chiaburu, and J.I. Menges, "Strategic use of emotional intelligence in organizational settings: Exploring the dark side," *Research in Organizational Behavior*, vol. 30 pp. 129–152, 2010.

139 R. Thaler, "Toward a positive theory of consumer choice," *Journal of Economic Behavior and Organization*, vol. 1, pp. 39–60, 1980.

140 N.N. Taleb, *Fooled by Randomness: The Hidden Role of Chance in Life and in the Markets,* 2nd Edition (New York: Random House, 2005).

141 *Ibid,* p. 8.

142 *Ibid,* p. 13.

143 L. D'Olimpio, "The trolley dilemma: would you kill one person to save five?" *The Conversation*, June 3, 2016; https://theconversation.com/the-trolley-dilemma-would-you-kill-one-person-to-save-five-57111

144 J.J. Thomson, "Killing, letting die, and the trolley problem," *The Monist*, vol. 59, pp. 204–217, 1976.

145 A. Saide and K. McCaffree, "A Paradox of Tolerance?" Skeptic Research Center, SPAS003, 2020; https://www.skeptic.com/research-center/reports/Research-Report-SPAS-003.pdf

146 M. Bendixen, "Denmark's selfish stance does nothing to help the global refugee crisis," *The Guardian*, January 27, 2016; https://www.theguardian.com/commentisfree/2016/jan/27/denmark-selfish-global-refugee-crisis-immigration

147 A. Kustov, "The parochial altruist: why voters are sceptical about immigration," The London School of Economics and Political Science, December 18, 2018; https://blogs.lse.ac.uk/brexit/2018/12/18/the-parochial-altruist-why-voters-are-sceptical-about-immigration/

CPSIA information can be obtained
at www.ICGtesting.com
Printed in the USA
BVHW041145250422
635276BV00009B/151